C+H
5⁰⁰

63-18741 (3-9-62)

POWER
IN MEN

POWER
IN MEN

By Joyce Cary

WITH AN INTRODUCTION
BY HAZARD ADAMS

University of Washington Press
Seattle • 1963

Contents

Introduction

I

Most books about politics live short lives. Time passes and we discover them in remainder sales. Then they languish for years on the dusty shelves of used book stores, sharing space with Lord So-and-So's memoirs, old campaign biographies, and Willkie's *One World*. This fate has not befallen the first edition of Joyce Cary's *Power in Men*, published in the fateful year of 1939. If any copies languished on the shelves, they have long since been picked up by book collectors and libraries. Why is this so? Cary's literary reputation is primarily responsible. Although real critical acceptance was slow enough in his lifetime, it has grown rapidly since his death in 1957. Whenever a novelist is acclaimed, scholarship and interpretation follow, and everything he has written takes on new importance. The best commentaries on a novelist's work are often his own discursive books and essays on apparently unrelated subjects, and this is certainly true of Cary's political writings, which include *The Case for African Freedom* (1941; rev. ed., 1944), *Process of Real Freedom* (1943), and *Britain and West Africa* (1946; rev. ed., 1947) as well as the present volume.

Power in Men, which is the first, most important, and most interesting of Cary's political books, sets forth the views out of which the later books arise; and these views are of a piece with Cary's book about art, *Art and Reality*. Cary's politics and aesthetic theory stem from a single vision of human nature. Students of Cary's fiction should welcome a new printing of *Power in Men* for what it tells us about the novels. Together with the book's interest as a document in the history of Liberal politics, this alone would save it from the dusty shelves, but it is perfectly capable of saving itself out of its own intrinsic imaginative power and humanity.

Like the later *Art and Reality, Power in Men* is a disarming book. First, it is not a long book, yet it faces up to an immense problem: What is an adequate definition of human freedom? Second, it faces this problem in a simple direct style, and does not labor under the burden of either public or private jargon. Its observations are based upon personal experience and are, as well, grounded upon considerable knowledge of philosophy. It is clear that Cary had read the great political philosophers who influenced Liberalism—romantics, anarchists, Marxists, all sorts of nineteenth-century radicals.[1] In fact, he had a knowledge of all shades of political opinion. Equally important, he understood that a political philosopher must constantly be aware of first principles. Cary is concerned with such things as epistemology and the nature of individual imaginative vision. In the background stands Immanuel Kant and further forward, William Blake. Cary writes also out of personal experience of the most intense sort. From 1916 to 1920 he was an officer of the British Nigerian service, deeply involved in a political situation—"managing people," as Chester Nimmo of the second trilogy calls it—where individuals were only emerging from primitivism.

II

Power in Men was the selection of the Liberal Book Club for May, 1939. Two books had preceded it in the series, and others were scheduled to follow. Ivor Brown's *Life within Reason*, issued in March, was the first. It was billed as "an examination of the failures and disappointments of democ-

[1] One political scientist has suggested to me that *Power in Men* has some affinities with the writings of Leonard Trevelyan Hobhouse, the great English Liberal sociologist.

racy in practice." In the light of the Liberal collapse of the twenties and thirties, Brown argued that "the hopes of the Liberal-minded concerning man as a Political Animal must have been based on a faulty psychology." His book was an attempt to "discover the mistakes of the too-optimistic democrat and to outline a more realistic attitude to the life, work and leisure of the contemporary citizen." There is detectable in this program a disillusionment with outworn slogans, an effort to escape from their abstract emptiness to an intimate concern with human beings as individuals. Indeed, in the Liberal writing of this time one senses a desperate need to discover new meanings for old words.

Ramsay Muir's *Future for Democracy* followed in April.[2] During the period between the great wars, Muir was perhaps the party's leading political philosopher. As early as 1920 he was trying to redefine freedom. In *Liberalism and Industry* he had written, "Real liberty is not mere absence of restraint, it is security in doing, by a man's free choice, all or any of the things that are worth doing."[3] In those words he partially anticipated, and may have influenced, Cary's own positive definition of liberty, which is the first principle of

[2] Nicholson and Watson were the publishers of the series.
[3] Quoted by Sir Henry Slesser, *A History of the Liberal Party* (London: Hutchinson and Co., 1944), p. 164.

Power in Men. Liberty is no longer adequately described in the old classical way but must be related to power—the positive power to help accomplish rational individual desires. In 1934, Muir had been the author of *The Liberal Way*, an inclusive survey of Liberal party policy. *Future for Democracy* was a restatement of Liberal principles in the more urgent atmosphere of 1939, when democracy was threatened by the advance of European totalitarianism. It actually represented little advance over the manifesto of five years before, the principles and means being nearly the same:

> The first is a belief in the sacredness of individual human personality, a belief that every unnecessary restriction of the expression of personality and of individual energy, is an evil which will sooner or later bring punishment upon the society which encourages or permits it. The second is a belief that the State, as the mouthpiece of the Community, can alone create the conditions which will make a reasonable life possible, but that these conditions must be such as to permit of and encourage the maximum development of individual powers [p. 309].

Cary would certainly have accepted these principles, though he proceeded in *Power in Men* to underline for emphasis "create," "encourage," and "powers." His book followed Muir's, and others were scheduled: *Leadership for Plenty* by Comyns Carr, *The Contours of Liberty* by Tom Harrisson,

INTRODUCTION

These Men Make Politics by A. J. Cummings, and
Ownership for All by Elliott Dodds. Cary's book
was, however, the last to reach print. The war
threatened, and the others remained ghosts of the
unborn, described briefly in Liberal Book Club
brochures. They would have grown up to attack
economic planning "by restriction for scarcity and
dearness," to analyze from information collected
by the Mass Observation Movement "the heights
and depths of those liberties we now enjoy," to
show to what extent the voter's destiny is bound
up with the failure or success of politicians as individuals, and to advocate the distribution, but not
the abolition, of private property.

The Liberal Book Club had begun with a distinguished committee and a list of patrons that
impresses one today as a sort of who's who of
Liberal opinion in the thirties. The officers of the
committee were the Marquis of Crewe, president,
and the Viscount Esher, chairman; its members
were A. J. Cummings, Dr. Margaret Deas, Roger
Fulford, J. B. Hobman, Harcourt Johnstone, E. E.
Kellett, Miss Margaret Kennedy, Mrs. Robert
Lynd, A. G. Macdonell, Sir Andrew McFadyean,
Mrs. C. F. G. Masterman, Osbert Sitwell, P. Gil-
christ Thompson, and Iolo Williams. The list of
patrons was, if anything, more interesting and included, among writers and artists alone, St. John

Ervine, Augustus John, J. M. Keynes, Compton Mackenzie, A. A. Milne, Gilbert Murray, and C. P. Snow. The club itself seems to have begun with high hopes typical of the political enthusiasm so often engendered in the thirties. It exhorted prospective members to read the books as they appeared and, with the assistance of the local Liberal agent, form discussion groups. These groups were to constitute the "spearhead of the local attack on the entrenchments of political reaction." The enemy was European fascism abroad and conservatism at home.

But the thirties were drawing to a close in tragedy, the Liberal party had not recovered from the schisms of the twenties, and the club's fond hopes were never to materialize. War was the answer to the fascists, and when peace was restored it was Labour which ousted the Conservatives from office. The Liberal party was not again to form a government. It may be said, I think, that the party's efforts to redefine liberty in the modern world, if not too little, were at least too late. The power to implement definition with political artistry and verve seemed to have been lost.

Nevertheless the first two books were well received by the press. The *Guardian* saw Brown's *Life within Reason* as an excellent introduction to liberalism. The *Observer* found it "readable" and "stimulating." The *Times Literary Supplement* was, in its bland way, pleased with both Mr. Brown and Mr. Muir. It greeted Cary's book somewhat more guardedly, however, with one of those reviews suggestive of hasty reading and little thought:

> There is a saying that Sir Banister Fletcher in his "History of Architecture on the Comparative Method" translated the Bible into Architecture. Mr. Cary in his arrangement of *Power in Men* seems to have attempted a similar task on behalf of Liberalism. Thus the Liberal Book Club choice for last month is divided into chapter and verse, which, if *Power in Men* is to become the philosophical basis for Liberalism reborn, is an excellent idea.
>
> This book is a statement of theory rather than an analysis of the Constitution as it works to-day. The author is on more relevant ground when discussing the dangers peculiar to democracy and its international organization. Especially valuable are the two chapters on education for liberty. Finally Mr. Cary is encouraging when he emphatically states that man is fundamentally a lover of freedom and that all tyrannies must eventually collapse because they are an unnatural state.[4]

That is the whole review. The first paragraph refers to Cary's habit of numbering his paragraphs (he does the same in *Art and Reality*). The observation is rather too trivial to take up half a review, particularly since the snide criticism implicit is

[4] No. 1950 (June 17, 1939), p. 351.

never given a firm basis. As for the second paragraph, since the reviewer has apparently not apprehended the central concerns of the book, he is hardly in a position to comment intelligently upon the relevance of particular chapters. It is clear, at any rate, that he does not have much patience with theory. I quote the review in full mainly because so many reviews of Cary's work were equally obtuse, and this one is therefore typical.

At the end of each month in those days the *Times Literary Supplement* recommended the best books of the month in a variety of fields. It was, I think, no disgrace to *Power in Men* that it was not in the June list, which under "politics" included *The Struggle for Peace* by Neville Chamberlain, *War, Peace, and Change* by John Foster Dulles, and Gunther's *Inside Asia*.

III

In *The Case for African Freedom* Cary tells us that *Power in Men* was not quite the sort of book that the Liberal committee had expected from him:

When I was asked in 1931 [?] by the Liberal Committee to write about politics, I at first refused. I had forgotten politics. I was deep in other studies, in philosophy, history and letters. But when I was offered a free hand to write what I liked, and began to con-

sider politics, I found to my own surprise and, I am
afraid, the surprise of the Committee, that the philosophy, since it dealt with realities, led, logically, to a
new state theory.[5]

This is somewhat overstated in two ways. First,
the Liberals prided themselves on their willingness
to entertain diverse views. In 1934, Muir had written: "It is at once the strength and the weakness
of the Liberal Party that it consists of Liberals
—that is to say, of people who insist upon exercis-
ing their own freedom of judgment."[6] Second, in
most respects Cary's book would seem, after all,
to support the Liberal program. What the Liberal
committee got and did not apparently expect (or
so Cary thought) was a positive philosophical
statement that could provide the groundwork for
specific measures.

Liberalism had been the dominant politics of
Victorian England. The Victorian age virtually
rose and declined as Liberalism rose and declined.
True, Lloyd George and Asquith presided at the
death agonies years after Victoria was dead, but
in a real sense Liberalism and the Victorian age
were one. The Liberal party grew out of the failure of the Whigs to move with the times. Essen-

[5] (Rev. ed.; London: Secker and Warburg, 1944), p. 12.

[6] *The Liberal Way: A Survey of Liberal Policy, Published
by the Authority of the National Liberal Federation* (London: George Allen and Unwin, 1934), p. 9.

tially the Whigs were aristocrats. Their original quarrel with the *status quo* was over the power of the monarchy. They championed the landowners, while the Tories thought of ownership as residing ultimately in the crown. Whiggery succeeded in greatly diminishing monarchial authority, but it failed to work for democratic reform. Its politics were governed by what was expedient to ensure the continued prosperity of the landed class. This is the reason why today we see no major difference between Whig and Tory unless we thrust ourselves imaginatively into the political situation of the early nineteenth century. One Liberal party historian writes:

> The only difference between [the Whigs] and the Tories was that they could read a little more clearly the signs of the times. They realized that the alternative to Reform was Revolution; Reform was their choice. But they believed they could make Reform so little effective that there would be no change of system for a long time.[7]

This was the Whig position in the early part of the century. Their unwillingness to change eventually spelled the death of the party, but they had been substantially correct about their ability to slow down change. After the Reform Act of 1832,

[7] Hamilton Fyfe, *The British Liberal Party: An Historical Sketch* (London: George Allen and Unwin, 1928), p. 25.

it was thirty-five years before a significant mass of the people gained the franchise under a Conservative government, which was soon to lose power to the first Liberal ministry of Gladstone.

Liberalism replaced Whiggery because too many people decided that the Whigs no longer had any principles to advance. And Labour eventually won the Liberal vote because Liberalism was unable in its own time of crisis to advance principles acceptable to the new age. Early in its life Liberalism came to be intimately associated with the Benthamite doctrine of the greatest happiness for the greatest number, but its first doctrine was that of *laissez faire* in economics. Liberals preached a minimum of government interference in personal affairs. In fact, they did not really consider governmental activities as other than interference. This attitude extended itself from economics, where free trade was the policy, to all life—art and religion included. The result was that happiness became associated with absence of restraint and synonymous with freedom.

The role of the state in this philosophy was somewhat ambiguous. Essentially its duty was to destroy all obstacles to freedom so conceived, in order that all men might pursue their individual aims. But for many Liberals this equalitarian aspect of the movement was not at all attractive. Whiggery had been a revolution of the aristocrat. Liberalism gave the wealthy middle class more power:

> The wealthy middle classes, especially the commercial and manufacturing sections, supported the Reform Bill because they wanted political power; they supported Free Trade because they wanted cheap food to keep down wages. Having secured these, their attitude towards further change was, for the most part, hostile. . . . All they wished government to do was to keep order, to leave trade free from all restrictions, to spend little, to tax lightly, and to preserve peace because peace was cheaper than war.[8]

That is perhaps a cynical view, but it is the view of a modern Liberal historian. Interest in a program of social reform which was to encompass the lower classes emerged only through the pressure of radical thought on what today we would consider a very reactionary attitude in both parties.

We notice in the principles of Liberalism a predominantly negative view of freedom, particularly in respect to the function of the state. Liberalism meant only to clear away obstructions, for that is all that it considered necessary to freedom. Negativism in a party dedicated to increasing human liberty eventually proved inadequate and contributed to its ruin. The twentieth century demanded a more dynamic conception of human possibility. Like the Whigs, whom they had re-

[8] *Ibid.*, pp. 26–27.

placed, the Liberals gave way to a movement that offered more positive goals. The definition of liberty as an absence seems to lie behind Ramsay Muir's remark in *The Liberal Way* that Liberalism in itself "largely disables the party from using the methods that seem to be most successful under our present electoral system" (p. 9). Therefore the Liberal party itself, because it conceived of freedom as an absence, operated in a state of comparative anarchy. This negativism appears again in Sir Henry Slesser's *History of the Liberal Party* (1944):

> . . . to the Liberal, authority is only to be supported as a regrettable necessity; for him, individual freedom is the *summum bonum;* whereas in the Conservative case (possibly also in the Socialist) external discipline and regulation have generally been regarded as inherently unobjectionable [p. 7].

In their negative conception of liberty, Liberals forgot or disregarded what might actively be desired. David Thompson has put it well:

> . . . beliefs of Liberalism were beliefs about means rather than about ends. They indicated how certain things could best be attained, without specifying very carefully what these things should be. The ends of maximum production in economics, of individual freedom in politics, of free association in society, were assumed, rather than considered.[9]

[9] *England in the Nineteenth Century, 1815–1914* (Harmondsworth, Eng.: Penguin Books, 1950), p. 227.

Twentieth-century life asked: How is wealth to be used and in what way is it best deployed? What good is freedom negatively defined to a man without the opportunity to live creatively?

In *Power in Men* Cary reconsiders principles. First, he rejects the old definition of liberty as absence of restraint. Under the tyranny of this definition, Liberalism, he feels, became reactionary. In Muir's *The Liberal Way* there is a lament for the collapse of Liberalism in the aftermath of World War I, the intraparty squabbles, the great depression, and the appearance of the European dictators. The tone is a shade reactionary because freedom is not newly defined:

> Liberalism—the belief in freedom of thought, freedom of enterprise, freedom of intercourse, and freedom in government—has been the chief guide of modern civilisation in all its progress during the last four centuries. The world seems to-day to be turning its back upon this guide; and the world has come near to ruin [p. 7].

Cary would surely have insisted that Muir was a wise and good man, and we know that Muir had written positively of freedom. But in some respects the statement above sounds like the lament of Tom Wilcher in *To Be a Pilgrim*. Cary says of Wilcher, also a wise and good man in his way:

> . . . he has grown up, like many Englishmen, Liberal by conviction but Conservative in heart. In him, that is, the attachments of sentiment, which are the per-

petual root of Conservative feeling, are stronger than the drive to adventure.[10]

Cary's positive definition of freedom finds its ultimate source in his assumptions about individual creative power and his belief that we do not merely perceive but actively make our reality. This belief is derived principally from the writings of William Blake, whose work was a dominant influence upon Cary from an early age, as can be seen from an examination of Cary's early poems and the use of Blake in *The Horse's Mouth*. Blake has been described as an apocalyptic humanist, and that description will serve; for it preserves the two aspects of Blake's vision—the secular and religious—as one. For Blake, the secular-religious distinction was as absurd as the distinction between body and soul. The body is simply that portion of the soul perceived by the five senses. The "religious" in Blake were the reactionary forces who attempt to control morality. Cary has a good deal to say about these people in his discussion of censorship in *Power in Men* (pp. 201ff.), and Blake would have approved of his remarks.

In Blake's vision, man either creates his own world within his imaginative being or allows the world to trap him within a prison of dead matter.

[10] *To Be a Pilgrim* (Carfax edition; London: Michael Joseph, 1951), p. 7.

If he succumbs to the latter, he dies into nightmare. The conservative in Tom Wilcher has fallen into such a sleep, from which the demon of his creative intelligence struggles to awaken him. *To Be a Pilgrim* verges upon dialogue between Wilcher's demon and the conservative angel of his reason. We may recall that in Blake angels are the passive who obey reason and devils are those active intelligences who follow their energies. The conservative in Wilcher sees Gulley Jimson as a dangerous devil, but the Liberal in him is not quite so sure. For the Liberal senses his vitality. Indeed Gulley Jimson is Cary's finest image of the creative intelligence in art, just as Chester Nimmo is creative man in politics.

It is not out of character for Jimson to quote from Blake in *The Horse's Mouth*. Jimson's imaginative eyes are constantly expanding in Blakean fashion to contain the world they perceive. At one point in Jimson's narrative these lines from Blake run through his mind:

> I stood in the streams
> Of Heaven's bright beams
> My eyes more and more
> Like a sea without shore
> Continued expanding.
> The Heavens commanding.[11]

[11] Quoted in *The Horse's Mouth* (Carfax edition; London: Michael Joseph, 1951), p. 223.

In both Blake and Cary imagination turns the cold inanimate world inside out. To put it another way, the whole world is pulled inside man through the doors of perception. Reality is to be made and used,[12]

> For every generated body in its inward form
> Is a garden of delight and a building of mag-
>   nificence [p. 41].

I mention all this because Cary's conception of freedom as power is based upon it. In *Power in Men* he often dismisses theories as "abstract," as the work of what Blake called the "passive that obeys Reason," human failure to surround experience with the body of imagination. Power to drag the world into oneself is the root of man's potential freedom. It is ultimate reality:

> [Liberty] belongs to ultimate reality. It is present in all purposive action, from the slightest muscular movement of any living creature to the grandest ideal construction of the poet or the artist [p. 7].

Power in men is real, while power in nations is derived. The state gathers its power from individuals and exists to increase, in turn, individual

---

[12] Both Wilcher and Nimmo speak of women they know as having "used religion." By this they are not being derogatory but praising the unity of their lives in which religion is not separated from other forms of action but is part of the total creation of their worlds. Religion lives in them; they are not contained by it.

power. The negative view of how the state can help men increase their power, which was the legacy of nineteenth-century Liberalism, stands in the way of democratic progress. There are, of course, dangers inherent in democracies, and Cary enumerates them: indecision in foreign affairs, industrial strife, lack of economic planning on a national scale and resultant waste, possible deadlocks in the division of power. But the primary block to progress is the outworn idea of liberty as an absence:

> . . . by teaching people false ideas about their relation to the state, by making them believe that their interests are necessarily opposed to all state action, they weaken their own cause and injure the power of the state [p. 153].

That the term "power of the state" seems to us today almost obscene indicates how deeply entrenched the traditional negative ideas of freedom and power actually are. But the state's true and enduring power is enhanced only when it actively helps man develop his creative capacities.

Since liberty is not an absence, it follows that you cannot, as Cary remarks in *The Case for African Freedom*,

> . . . give liberty to people by a wave of the hand, as you throw open a cage. If you attempted it you would find that your victim, like the cage birds turned loose, would only injure or poison themselves. They would

be lucky if, more or less damaged, they found at last another cage, however small, to creep into [p. 26].

These words, written in a later book, but implied in the pages of *Power in Men*, accurately comment on events in Cuba and the Congo today and would seem to provide a good means of measuring the colonial policies of the great powers. How much real liberty did their regimes help to *make*? Did they simply open the door for caged birds?

Cary insists that if the state educates its children and actively supports its artists and scientists it will increase its own strength. In his optimism about the powers of education Cary's Liberalism is perhaps most clearly displayed. A cynic might say that his remarks are apparently those of someone who has never been a professional teacher. Whatever view we take, it is worthwhile to remember that Cary is speaking of a *liberal* education: The state must educate without defining what it specifically desires. Should it begin to make definitions it will end by insisting on uniformity of thought and action. Above all, it must not define man dogmatically. Indeed it should not define him at all except as a "unique center of creative power." Man is neither a political nor an economic nor a rational animal. In Cary's view, man is perhaps nearer to the "animal symbolicum" of Ernst Cassirer; he is a creature who *makes* his reality: "He is moved by sympathies, tastes, faiths which have nothing to do with politics or cash" (p. 35).

This is one of the reasons that Cary begins his prefatory essay to *Prisoner of Grace* as follows: "The difficulty of a book about a politician is that people will tend to read it as a book about government. But politics is the art of human relations, an aspect of all life."[13] His view is amply demonstrated in the second book of the so-called political trilogy, *Except the Lord*, in which the character of the political artist Chester Nimmo is shown to be intimately bound up with religious attitudes formed in his youth. In fact, religion plays, if anything, a larger part in Nimmo's memoir than politics. A good many readers of the trilogy have, however, been unable to make a judgment about Nimmo that adequately admits the importance of his religious experience and the extent to which it colors his actions. As a result they have not fully understood his motivations and have thought him more shallow and generally less admirable than he really is. At the same time, and for this reason, they have not quite understood Cary's view of politics.

The moral is that people cannot be shoved into simple categories. Life is a unity rather than a mul-

[13] (Carfax edition; London: Michael Joseph, 1954), p. 5.

tiplicity, and no theory of politics can therefore overlook any aspect of man's creativity without impoverishing itself. The scientific myth of mechanical man must be opposed by a more inclusive vision. Scientists should not say: "Man is a mechanism, and all evils of the world arise because he does not work properly or in accord with other mechanisms" (p. 19). Cary vigorously attacks this view. It is Blake's rage against abstraction brought up to date: Any single vision of man results in the oppression of the whole man.

IV

Cary's refusal to limit politics to politics helps account for the cool reception given to his novels in the thirties and, to a certain extent, even later. Reviewers obstinately misunderstood what he was trying to do. *The African Witch*, one of his best works and one which *Power in Men* particularly helps us to understand, fell victim to the naïve and popular view that the novel must be political and polemic according to some easily identifiable attitude. Searching for Cary's party line in an apparently political novel, Cary's critics misinterpreted his aim and overlooked the fact that politics in Cary always emerge from and plunge back into metaphysics and epistemology. Cary was himself aware of the problem when, looking back, he wrote his prefatory essay to the Carfax edition of *The African Witch*. What really interests him, he tells us, is the fundamental question of all politics:

> . . . what do men live by? What makes them tick and keeps them ticking;[14] and if you answer love and hate, curiosity, ambition, duty and pride, you are already deep, whether you like it or not, in metaphysics, in the science of the soul, or whatever synonym you may choose for that central activity.[15]

This remark applies to all his novels. He follows it with a clear analysis of why novels about the human imagination in politics are often misread:

> In practice, as every writer knows, whatever he writes, will be somewhere misunderstood. This book, for instance, was at once treated, even by serious officials, as an attack on their administration; by street corner politicians, as a work on the colour-bar. True, in 1936 political ideas and political arguments were a good deal more innocent than they are to-day. Most of the discussion was in the style of Reading without Tears. A cat is on the mat. The Empire is naughty. Primitive savages are good—but European civilization is corrupt. . . . What is startling to anyone who has done a real political job, is the naivity and cocksureness of popular slogans about government [pp. 11–12].

[14] One can see how deeply entrenched the myth of mechanical man really is because, although he opposes the myth, Cary himself employs a mechanical metaphor to describe man.

[15] (London: Michael Joseph, 1951), pp. 9–10.

Even in the fifties, with publication of his second "political" trilogy, Cary was attacked in a review for his failure to understand early twentieth-century British politics. I do not see how this argument could have been sensibly put forward. It is likely that the reviewer forgot that as a novelist Cary was *making* situations rather than recording them from life and that his real concern with political action was to portray it as a projection of the creative imaginations of his people. Nor was it up to him to side with one or another political sloganist. In fact, the trilogy is deeply concerned with the hollowness of slogans.

Imaginative power being the fundamental subject of Cary's fiction, we would expect remarks about it in *Power in Men* to be related to the novels; our expectation is not disappointed. The prefatory essays that Cary wrote for the Carfax edition provide the link, if indeed one is needed. In the preface to *An American Visitor*, we see how a commentary on Cary's novel moves in one direction toward the political principles enunciated in *Power in Men* and in the other toward emphasis upon the creative imagination of his characters. It is characteristic of him to return from political speculation to the "unique center of free power":

> I was asked about the American visitor. So what? And this is all the answer one can give. There is no rule.

poverty to a position of prominence in the Liberal
war cabinet of Lloyd George and is turned out by
the voters in the Liberal collapse of 1922. In his
career we note the influence that played upon Liberalism throughout the late Victorian age. Most
abiding is the evangelical faith Nimmo inherited
from his father. I wonder if it is Cary's little joke
that the elder Nimmo predicted the end of the
world for a day in 1868. That was the year in which
the first Liberal government came to power. The
millennium? Though there were periods in which
Nimmo had apparently lost his faith ("neglected"
is probably a more accurate word), evangelical
Christianity was an abiding influence upon him, as
it was upon Liberalism. But evangelicalism was
mixed with strange ingredients. As a young man
Nimmo heard a political speaker he could not forget—an Italian disciple of Proudhon (see *Power
in Men*, pp. 54–55) who became a lieutenant of
Bakunin and ultimately a sort of Tolstoyan anarchist (see pp. 56–57). This man despised organized religion as tyrannical suppression. Then
Nimmo met and worked for a Marxist labor leader
named Pring. But in an 1870 strike he broke with
him over ways and means: "Pring loved power too
much and men not at all."[17] Pring was, in other
words, an abstractionist. Nimmo loved power

[17] *Except the Lord* (London: Michael Joseph, 1953), p. 272.

too, but something within him fought against a leader who reduced men to the abstract.

Later, when he had been elected to Parliament, Nimmo, following Lloyd George, defended the Boers and gained a reputation for pacifism popular in his evangelically inclined constituency. But when England moved toward war with Germany, he remained in the war cabinet (much to the disgust of some of his supporters), favored conscription and the trial of the Kaiser, and seemed, all told, to have rejected his earlier position. In the disastrous election of 1922 he was turned out with his party, and he was defeated again in 1924. Finally he becomes Lord Nimmo.

Nimmo's apparent shifts of principle reflect dominant changes in the Liberal politics of his time, caused by shifts in the sources of power. From another point of view the changes represent different aspects of Liberalism coming into domination in party and individual. Cary insists that people and not abstract theory make life, and people change their minds. As an individual Nimmo seems to contain symbolically the party to which he belonged.

From his former wife Nina's account in *Prisoner of Grace*, Nimmo would seem to be the typical evangelical Liberal: "Freedom for Chester was the answer to every problem. It meant for him,

Let God provide—don't get in his way" (p. 83).
But this does not adequately sum him up, and no
one knows that better than Nina does. Early in his
career Nimmo seems to have striven in the direction of the more positive definition of freedom set
forth in *Power in Men*. In his memoir he is gently
critical of the old definitions, accepted as the facts
of life by people of his father's station:

> Many a girl in the bad times passed in a year from
> bridehood and motherhood to the workhouse or the
> streets. For the men would move away following the
> work where it was to be found. They were expected to
> do so. Was it not a law of the economists that labour
> seeks its market at the place of production? So the
> children of starving cottagers had poured into the
> towns for work in the new factories, and so when some
> industry was ruined the workers would travel hundreds
> of miles to some newer and more prosperous trade. . . .
>
> Such economics in those days were not only the
> tenets of the rich, I have heard them from the lips of
> poor men. My own father, as far as he took the least
> interest in a subject so remote from his own deeper
> preoccupations, held something of the kind. They were
> indeed implicit in the very centre of the evangelical
> creed, that all was in the hands of the all-wise provi-
> dence [pp. 68–69].

Nimmo reacted at least partially against the
economic and religious naïveté which seemed to
dictate this state of affairs, but more against the
economics than against the religion. He never

really rejected his religious upbringing. Instead he supported economic plans that reflected the best of it. Even during a period of comparative doubt he wrote to his wife:

> True religion centres in the family—for the Protestant, priesthood resides in every parent responsible for a child's upbringing. That is why we are bound to stand for any state policy that can secure the family unit as a unit [p. 104].

Economics had nearly ruined his own family. It brought the death of his mother, led to the death of his sister, and sorely afflicted the lives of all the others. This experience and the evangelical principle of family solidarity led to Nimmo's support of pensions and the dole.

Despite his radicalism Nimmo failed, as did his party, to secure the needed definition of freedom before power slipped from his hands. The party split, and only the hollow oratory of old slogans remained. Cary was well aware of the state of affairs in the party when he wrote *Power in Men*, and he tried to offer a remedy. Indeed Liberal intellectuals were generally dissatisfied with old formulae. In his history of the party, published in 1944, Sir Henry Slesser found the concluding words of Ramsay Muir's *Liberalism and Industry* (1920) quite inadequate:

In conclusion, the author, not very convincingly, asserts that "modern Liberalism is not merely helpless and bewildered in face of the problems which surround us." Those not in the Liberal Assembly may be less sure.[18]

If Nimmo did not quite succeed in making new meanings (he had after all helped to put the old ones into action), he was nevertheless a man of power. Nimmo had decided that the Marxist Pring loved power "too much," but Cary knew that all creative men love power and that their creativity is their power. In the prefatory essay to *Prisoner of Grace*, Cary wrote:

I am not pretending that Nimmo was a completely admirable character. There are few such anywhere in the world. He is an egotist like most successful politicians. Probably no man would give himself to that craft, certainly he would not succeed in it, without a great deal of conceit. . . .

An acute American critic said that Gulley Jimson of the Horse's Mouth was a politician in art, and Nimmo an artist in politics. This is true and penetrating in so far that both are creative minds in the world of a perpetual creation. They are inventing unique answers to problems that are of necessity always new.

The same critic, to my surprise, said that Wilson was a greater man than Roosevelt. To me Wilson has always seemed like a stiff, dogmatic person, applying formulae to life; Roosevelt, the artist creator, improvis-

[18] *A History of the Liberal Party*, p. 165.

ing as he went, a genius in handling the ever-changing complexity of human affairs. What Wilson lacked was precisely the creative imagination, and the want of it ruined his policy [p. 6].

Cary judged these politicians by their imaginative power.

It is remarkable how often the word "power" turns up in crucial places in the trilogy. Nina remarks of her husband that early in his career, "he knew already a good deal about power" (p. 107). In his own memoir Nimmo tells of watching a play at a fair, which he and his sister attended against his father's religious scruples. He and his sister "burned with our new imaginations and discoveries" (p. 97). He was particularly entranced by one of the actors, who, "had revealed a fearful, an astonishing power—one that entranced my boy's soul not only by its imposing solitary glory, but perhaps even more profoundly by its defiance" (p. 99). After this experience he did not enter a theater for more than thirty years. Yet even as he distrusted power of this sort, it continued to fascinate him—"power that I had seen exercised by my father—though in a lesser degree—the spell of the orator." He remembers himself in the early days as a "rough dirty boy" who spoke "as in spite against his lot," but with a "vision of glory by means of the spoken word" (p. 111). It is to his credit that he recognizes, with an ambivalence that did not prevent him from taking decisive actions, the dangers of hollow words, of those dead abstractions produced by the Blakean mental "mills." In the mill, life leaks out of language and all that remains is dogmatic law.

Telling of one of the crises in his political career, his wife remarks that he began to speak of "managing people" (p. 148). A step past this, one speaks of managing masses and forgets actual human life. Nimmo seems to sense that the drive toward political power can take such a direction and actually dissipate power unless it is infused with constant imaginative effort attached to concrete experience. In the trilogy, Nimmo's women—his mother, his sisters, his wife—represent to him the sources of his own imaginative power. He remembers his older sister Georgina living by "imagination and experience":

> Georgina admiring the curtain stuff at Slapton, under my surprised and contemptuous gaze, was obeying a more profound impulse of social conscience than I. She did not even notice the conception of class loyalty which to me was law [p. 216].

So at heart Nimmo is a very gentle abstractionist with a religious devotion to his unfaithful wife, and she is indeed for him the incarnation of his imaginative existence. There is a very important

chapter of *Except the Lord* (chap. 47) in which
Nimmo describes Nina to us. The situation is
complicated because he is dictating the memoir to
her and she is no longer his wife, having divorced
him and married her cousin. Nimmo has come to
her house, probably faked a heart attack, and
stayed on to be near her. The woman he describes
seems hardly the one who speaks directly to us in
Prisoner of Grace. His description of her is full
of oratorical mannerism and the cliché-filled in-
sincerity of the politician. Furthermore, Nimmo
is obviously trying to win her back with flattery
and by playing upon her sympathy. The description is supposed to have an effect upon her as well
as upon the reader, and the two effects are supposed to be different. The description is mislead-
ing to us because it conveniently disregards some
of the least pleasant aspects of their marriage. But
in another sense it is a sincere effort, and it con-
tains truth:

> Last week I had a heart attack, to-day, the ninth of
> April, is the first on which I have been allowed out
> of bed. I sit here by the window and look at those
> fragile buds of spring that may outlive me, yet never
> have they been more delightful to my eyes, more
> powerful with the grace of courage and hope. And she
> who has been my wife, my nobler self, the close and
> secret comrade of my darkest hours, who has given to
> me more than her youth, her life and loyalty—the per-

petual knowledge of a truth that is truth's very substance, the faith of the heart—who has sacrificed all to
me over thirty years—sits before me, pen in hand. . . .

Her once most beautiful hair is grey; the face which
charmed London in its most splendid years is worn and
lined with long suffering; but never has she been more
lovely in my sight, never has her presence and support
been more necessary to this poor atomy.

One flesh, how magic and how terrible is this phrase
to those who love—one flesh for good and for evil—
one flesh and one soul in which the nerves, the sympathies, speak as across a common heart, with the meanings not to be expressed in words.

She is part of me as I of her—she is my woman's
part. . . [p. 214].

He remembers also his sister's admonition:

. . . and Georgina wondered and raged at me and said,
"Everything isn't politics." And I understood how little
I knew of the real world in which people actually live,
and make their lives [p. 215].

In the light of Nina's own story and her view of
Nimmo we cannot help thinking, as we read these
astonishing passages, "Why, the old conniver!"
But there is truth in Nimmo's ingenious improvisa-
tion. In the world Nimmo has created, Nina is his
true Blakean emanation, the body of his ideal desire, the muse of his politics. We notice, even as he
tells us all this, that he is well aware of "meanings
not to be expressed with words." It is part of
Nimmo's politics that some things are better left

unsaid, but there is another meaning in his statement. It is his tragedy and the tragedy of all life that words do not suffice. In *Art and Reality* Cary remarks that poets have complained about words for thousands of years. Nimmo, who knows their power, recognizes as well their inadequacy. It is important to the significance of the novel that Nimmo, who speaks in clichés to flatter his wife, also distrusts clichés.

Nimmo's women have been for him the image of real life and experience which refurbishes his words and by which his drive for power is held back from total abstraction. Without these women his language deadens and loses meaning. What we have seen in his flattery of Nina is an ingenious and desperate effort to re-establish his relationship to his muse. This explains his religious devotion to Nina, which has seemed to her at times ludicrous and embarrassing. His desperation to hold to her all through their curious marriage, the deceit he employs, the refusal to admit verbally her unfaithfulness, the final ruse of the heart attack—all reflect his need and desire to maintain his spiritual integrity. Nina's defection from Nimmo comes, incidentally, as the Liberal party collapses and Nimmo himself is defeated at the polls. It is as if at the loss of his "woman's part" he has lost the power to be an artist in politics. He is still a Liberal, but he senses that something is gone. The youth of the nation have been deceived by words, and the simple evangelical faith of his father is fast disappearing:

> The world itself is young, we are but little removed from the time when writing was a wonder, when any written speech was magic. Words printed in books—Rousseau, Proudhon, Owen, Marx, what power they can wield. But it is the power of sorcerers—the spell they cast is abracadabra. And the fruit of their sorcery is egotism and madness, war and death [p. 274].

There is not space to consider all the ramifications of this complex passage. Behind it stand his father's preaching, the actor at the fair, and his own youthful vision of power. Nor can we now consider how much the passage reflects Nimmo's disillusion, how much it is a calculated statement meant to trap us into seeing before us a simple man. Words have been Nimmo's power. Old and out of office, estranged from his muse, he complains of words as if he were Faust sitting in his study. He does so because he knows the hollowness of old slogans and their danger and because he can no longer find the inspiration to invent with his old power new and necessary meanings:

> To bind man's future in a coil of words is to put an iron cage on the tender limbs of a child. I do not repent of the liberalism which inspired that great government in which I served, I do not stand in a sheet, much less a

winding sheet, for our creed—for tolerance, for freedom, for private rights, yea, even for private property—
tolerance which is room to grow, private rights and
private property which are the only defence against
public wrong and public breach of trust [p. 276].

Nimmo is a skeptical romantic, now a bit past the
moment of his power; and yet he knows that unless man aims at the life of the soul "all his achievement will be a gaol or a mad-house, self-hatred,
corruption and despair" (p. 284). That Nimmo
cannot quite say anything simply and without
oratorical flourishes is at the center of Cary's novel.
That Nimmo's own words do not seem quite
genuine leads us, oddly enough, away from dwell-
ing upon his deceitfulness to perceiving his underlying tragic brilliance. Nimmo, the man of power,
reaches the zenith, and we discover that it is pre-
cariously close to the nadir. Nimmo's final visions
of experience are more than his language can contain, and we sense the content dropping from his
words even as this sense of the failure of words
becomes for him part of the truth he learns. On
the surface his protestations of Liberal faith sound
like the turning of a political prayer wheel. Reading the manifestoes of the Liberal party in the twenties and thirties has somewhat the same effect.

In *Except the Lord*, Cary would have us read
behind outdated babel to the glory and tragedy of

the birth, life, and decline of a political vision. Nimmo is not, as a recent critical book has described him, merely a "wangler" but a man of imaginative power. In his old age his power is not quite adequate to a renewed imaginative effort in politics, nor is the power of his party. It is probably true that each political vision lives and ebbs and we should not expect a new and unique imaginative effort from a man or generation of men which has already given us one. This is one of the reasons that Cary is sympathetic with Nimmo, just as he admires so many of the radical thinkers of the nineteenth century even as he criticizes their theories.

In *Power in Men*, Cary makes an analysis of what meanings are necessary to political creativity. The argument of *Power in Men* is therefore relevant to the action of the trilogy, and in the broadest possible and most fundamental ways. That *Power in Men* and the novels rise in different directions from the same source should make us more alert in either case to what Cary's vision of the human situation ultimately is. For the reader, to seek that source from either direction is a pleasure, and the discovery a truth.

Thus we know that we have liberty exactly as we know that we are ourselves. A man who said, "But I am not a self, I am nobody" may fairly be asked,

"Who, then, is giving this opinion and what is it worth?"

Of one who denies liberty, we may ask, "If you have no power to judge anything, what is your judgment worth?" [p. 256].

HAZARD ADAMS

Dublin, Ireland
1963

CHAPTER I

Power in Men, as Liberty

1. The weakest child has power and will. Its acts are its own. It can be commanded, but it need not obey. It originates each least movement. It is an independent source of energy which grows with its life and ends only with its death.

This power is creative. In man it has created all the machines, all the states, the wealth, arts, and civilization in the world.

A man's power is different in kind from state power. A nation is more than living men, but without living men it would not exist. Men existed before nations. The power in the man is real, but the power of a nation is derived. It is the creation of men.

2. This creative power is free. It can be encouraged, strengthened, and directed, but it cannot be treated like mechanical power. A machine cannot refuse to do exactly what is expected of it, but even slaves will not work if they do not choose. If they cannot murder their

1

masters or escape, their last act of independence is to die.

3. Primitive tribes ruled by traditional law do not dream of questioning the law, but they will break it. Some man is arrested for witchcraft. His family dare not protect him. They are even officious to help the prosecution. But one of them, perhaps the man's wife, in the ceremonial and traditional silence of the ordeal, will suddenly scream out that he is innocent and that the jujuman is a murderer. Such a woman expects to be killed, and probably she will be killed. But her action takes no care of a law far stronger than anything known among civilized peoples. It is completely original and free.

Anyone who knows primitive people knows how frequently they show this independence ; how often in a village, when all the elders are agreed upon some point, one, possibly among the humblest, will suddenly make his objection and stand to it. The elders will abuse him or say, "He's always like that, he does it to show off." But that is to say that the man feels and acts like an independent person.*

This free power of action is true liberty, and the feeling of it, which must be as old ɩs self-

---

* See Malinowski in his book *Crime and Custom in Savage Society* for this perpetual conflict between private will and traditional law.

consciousness itself, is the source of the idea of liberty. Among primitive peoples it has, of course, very small political effect. Its creation is chiefly in art which, for the most part, is not kept or recorded—in songs, improvised poetry, dancing, drum music, and conversation, the chief art among all illiterates. But it is the perpetual running fountain and source of all liberty.

4. Liberty is usually defined as absence of restraint. This is what it seems and this has been the idea of it in political theory from very early times. But this theory has led to confusion, because one man's liberty is another man's restraint. For instance, a walker's liberty to cross the road is prevented by a motorist's liberty to drive as fast as he likes without being stopped. The policeman who stops the motorist destroys his liberty. But he gives liberty to the walker.

In this idea of liberty, all interference is wrong. So that it is a crime against liberty to arrest a pickpocket or to prevent a ship-owner from sending out his men in a rotten ship to get insurance money. But lovers of liberty were the first to say that the ship-owner was a criminal.

They were therefore in the position of saying, "We defy all restraint, which is a crime against liberty—but this crime must be committed."

3

5. All who think of liberty as absence of restraint are bound to fall into this confusion. They demand government action to protect liberty from restraint, but they want to abolish government as the chief restraint on liberty.* Thus serious university professors with conservative sympathies sit down in their studies to write pure anarchist theory.

Meanwhile each new law appears like a triumph over liberty, and people who find any good in the law ask what good liberty is.

State action has enormously increased in the last forty years, so that the very idea of liberty has come into contempt. Dictators laugh at it and theorists pick it to pieces. If anyone should say, "I am writing a book about liberty," his friends smile indulgently and cannot even invent a polite comment. They think that there is nothing to be said about liberty except old-fashioned sentiments or the contradictions which long ago exploded themselves.

Yet the very people who are most cynical at liberty's expense long for liberty, and while they say that there is no such thing possible for men, they feel secretly that it is every man's right.

6. If liberty be described as an absence of restraint, it is, of course, nothing. It is a

---

* "Perfect liberty is the total absence of government," Seeley, *Introduction to Political Science*. Macmillan, 1896.

vacuum, like the space of the old physics which was supposed to give liberty to the stars, and it breeds as many anomalies. It leads directly to despotism, which is uncontrolled liberty in a single ruler, and anarchy, which is unrestrained liberty in a single man. There is no vacuum in the real world of men and things.* We see men in open space, but the emptiness is an illusion, and men, like stars, move in and by power.

7. A critic has said, "Creative power in man is real, but so is absence of restraint. Why call the first liberty instead of the other ?"

It is quite true that absence of restraint exists as an idea, but only as an idea. It is not real. Even as an idea it cannot exist except in relation to power. Restraint itself is inconceivable without power to restrain. Absence of restraint is but the shadow of their conflict. A man who gets up from sickness may rejoice in liberty. What has really happened to him ? His strength has been restored. A prisoner released from gaol has escaped from restraint, but what he feels and enjoys is the power to do what he likes.

8. Definitions have no value unless they mean something real tested by facts. What do

* Vacuum here, of course, meaning nothingness ; not merely absence of air, which occurs within all atoms, including those of the air gases.

men mean by liberty ? How do they act to get it ?

In 1832 England was full of men demanding liberty. But they were not asking for the removal of restraint. They wanted votes, political power.

Take this from history. "But in 1687 the people, accustomed to liberty, were formidable to the new absolutist king." If you interpret this "the people, accustomed to absence of restraint," you form the idea of spoilt children or a disorganized mass, not formidable to anyone. You falsify real history, and if you are a statesman you suffer for it. But if you say "the people, accustomed to power, were formidable," you hit upon the real facts—the actual power of certain whig lords in country districts and the apprentice boys organized in the city bands against a king's power.

Everywhere in real history, in real affairs, it will be found that men in seeking what they call liberty seek to increase or defend their personal power. But this power is free. It is not mechanical power, but free creative power. Therefore all those who nowadays, forgetting liberty, reckon labour-force, man-power, as if it were a mechanical unit, to be controlled by a lever, are equally abstract in thought with the old theorists. They are dealing not in facts but formulas. Man-power, in the man, is free. It is liberty. It will therefore act in a manner totally different from that of a machine. For a man is a living soul and a machine is dead.

9. A dead man feels the weight of no law. By the old notion of liberty, he is the freest man in the world. In fact he has no liberty at all. Liberty is not an absence but a power. It is the power in man to do what he likes so far as his power can reach.

Liberty is not a sentiment or a word to be misused by theorists and ignored by practical men. It is real in the strictest and profoundest sense. It belongs to ultimate reality. It is present in all purposive action, from the slightest muscular movement of any living creature to the grandest ideal construction of the poet or the artist.

Liberty is creation in the act. It is therefore eternal and indestructible. Whether man recognizes it for what it is or calls it what it is not, it is always at work. The contempt and abuse of its enemies can no more destroy it than they can dissolve being itself. It is and remains. But a false idea of its nature can hinder its action, as a bad map can do more to delay explorers than none at all.

10. Power is in people ; and this is true of all states, whatever their government. In

some the people's power is chiefly industrial, it has small political function ; in others it rules. But it is everywhere. To say that the people have power in all states is different from saying that despotism exists in all governments. For the people's power is natural power, indestructible by any political accident. Like the natural ground beneath a fortress, it is waiting in mere course of time to swallow its master. Wherever a tyranny falls, democracy is seen.

Sometimes it is seen only for a moment between the fall of one despot and the rise of another, like the lie of the natural ground when some earthquake throws down a city. It appeared so, for a few years, in a thousand Greek and Italian cities after the defeat or ruin of tyrants, in revolutionary France between the kings and the emperors, in Manin's Venetian republic. It is always there, because beneath the structure of the despotic state are men possessing their own power and responsible for its use in social relations.

11. The increase of that power by any means, for instance by education or industrial skill, increases the total power of the individual ; and this actual power—even though in a despotic state the people may have no greater acknowledged power—at once presses upon the

government.   Democracy makes itself noticed.
It has political effect.

Democracy   works   always   from   below.
Political power does not generate democracy ;
democracy grows into political power.   The
industrial revolution of the eighteenth century,
in England, came before the political revolution
of 1832.   The increasing wealth of the German
people in the nineteenth century forced the social
reforms of the late Empire and prepared for the
Republic.   The Russian peasantry, illiterate,
divided, was never dangerous to the Tsars.
It was the middle class which made revolution.
The destruction of that class has repressed
Russian democracy.   It will revive with the
new schools, the new industrial organization.
Each new factory is a weapon in its hand.*
It advances with the power of millions.   Each
step in prosperity is followed by a new pressure
upon the state.   The process can be seen in
continuous action throughout the world.   The
more prosperous a people, the more demanding,
and   the   more   democratic   the   government.
That is why modern autarchies,† where the
people are literate and possess high industrial
skill, are different in kind from the despotisms
of the eighteenth century.   Louis XIV could

* See para. 132 : Economic Organization.
† I use this word for the modern form of despotism.

think of the French nation as his hereditary estate. The people were his children or his slaves. He was surrounded with the ritual of a god-king and his proclamations spoke with divine aloofness and grandeur. Victories were his victories and he spoke of "my army, my triumphs." But a modern dictator, at least in Europe, is obliged to play the demagogue. He tries to please and flatter the people, and when he makes a conquest he attributes it to the nation or the national spirit.

12. The reason is that though dictators have more power, so have the people, and that the distinction between political and other kinds of power is not real. It is only a classification. The political power of dictators rests upon productive power in the people. But that, in the last resort, is independent of the dictator's will. So are the people's minds, and if they have got by education the power to think and judge for themselves, the knowledge of what revolutions have done and the imagination to plot and to organize, they are greatly to be feared by anyone who threatens or injures their positive liberty. If the fall of wages or rising prices of food take from them some power of enjoyment, they become formidable, and the dictators must persuade them quickly that they are getting some other advantage or avoiding some worse injury.

Thus democracy swells up even beneath dictators —not as formerly beneath the old patriarchal kings with the slow growth of mountains, a foot in a thousand years, but with volcanic speed and force ; and at every new political earthquake, the democracy that appears below is more definite in form and massive in its bulk. All modern states are trying to build earthquakeproof. But every modern state, liberal or despotic, that organizes for production puts more power in the hands of the people, and that power is sooner or later used as a complete power, political as well as economic. Thus real liberty grows, and with it, either hidden or open, real democracy. It may not show itself for a long time. It disappears from the politics of the day and politicians forget it, despise it, or ask if it will ever be seen again. The dictators laugh at it and anxious liberal statesmen write of the crisis of democracy ; but it is always there.

Democracy has political accidents, but it cannot disappear. In the modern state it is unlikely that it can even be diminished for more than a few years of disorganization.

13. Democracy, therefore, like liberty, of which it is made, is real and indestructible. As liberty is the creative power of man, indivisible and unique, so democracy is power in many

11

men combining together in society, according to its forms, and tending always, by the increase of that individual power, towards political authority. A democratic government is rulership in the people. It is natural government, as liberty is natural power.

It follows that, just as the autarch in defying liberty sets himself against a real force, so the individual in defying organized society or collective power opposes a positive force. The man by himself, whether ruler or subject, must reckon with liberty, which is power always in action. Unique power in the man, as liberty, does not mean that he has prescriptive rights superior to state right or social right, but only that, in actual politics, all societies tend towards democracy ; that is, organization for private or distributed power ; as against the autarchy, which is organization for centralized power. This process takes place whether men will it or not, and it is often quite as dangerous to the actual existence of a state as beneficent to individuals within it while the state holds together.

CHAPTER II

Liberty of Mind

14. The old definition of liberty has never applied to freedom of the mind. Those who defined liberty as an absence saw clearly that freedom was real. Man, they said, had moral freedom, which was a real thing, and some gave him also free will.*

"Free will" is an ambiguous term, but the moral freedom certainly exists. As Kant pointed out, every time a man says or thinks "I ought to do so-and-so," he assumes that he has a real, independent power. He assumes liberty of judgment. If he were a machine he could not blame himself for any crime, and none could justly expect from him any good act or punish any bad one.

This argument is important in metaphysics and in the theory of liberty, but it is still abstract. It tells us nothing about any specific person. All men, from a Hottentot to Socrates, have freedom in this sense, just as they have liberty.

* See note at end, para. 290.

13

But there is a great difference in the amount of their liberty and none in their moral freedom.

Yet we mean a difference between Socrates and his judges when we say that he was free from prejudice and that they were bound by it. He had spent his life trying to know truth and to form his judgment upon facts ; they took account only of traditional law.

This is not a moral distinction or even one of goodness. Galileo's judges and Galileo all had moral freedom. They were learned and good men and they acted upon a sense of duty. But it was useless for Galileo to argue with his judges that the earth moved, because they were not permitted by their faith, at that time, to believe it. Their minds were not free.

15. This, then, is a final distinction between minds : that some are open to new truth and welcome it ; but some are closed to new truth and crush it if they can. The first is scientific ; the other dogmatic. A scientist may be dogmatic, but he would deny it like a crime. A dogmatist who allowed new truth to puzzle or break a dogma would feel guilty towards his ruler, whether church or state. So that philosophers and scientists, though they have continually abused each other and made dogmas of their hypotheses, have never set up a lasting tyranny. Their appeal is still to reason and

facts, which anyone can use against them and which cannot be hidden. Their dogmas and their rancours die with them, and if there is anything true or useful in their creeds it is snatched up by a hundred pioneers cutting out their own empires of the free mind.

This is the quality of freedom, that all its good comes in time to good use and all its bad is dredged away. But freedom and liberty by themselves are not values. They are only the ground of value. A man can have a mind free from prejudice, and liberty of action, and choose to act badly. We do not say that all free-minded men are good or that all good men are free-minded. Many great saints have been full of prejudices and hatred for truth. But without freedom even saints do evil and without liberty in people all states, however strong, must fall.

16. States go to great expense in order to obtain judges free from prejudice. All practical men in science, engineering, politics need this freedom. It is essential not only to a man's own achievement but also to progress. A savage has moral freedom and natural liberty, but he is blocked in every path of thought or experiment by superstition or false belief. Palæolithic man had the same brain as the modern. Among the millions inhabiting the earth fifty thousand years ago there must have

been scores as brilliant in genius as the greatest among those who fill the books for a short two thousand since history began. But it took them much longer than that to perfect the stone axe. Primitive races do not lack intelligence but freedom. They are crushed and bound by false ideas derived from past authority, and are stultified by the traditional creed that such ideas are superior to truth. They are taught to reject freedom of mind, and therefore their brains are almost useless to them. The power of the mind is the most important part of liberty. It has added to natural liberty all the vast power of modern organization. Freedom in the mind is therefore the ground and means of liberty. A man must free his mind before he can act effectively in the real world. So far as he is free will he make full use of liberty.

17. Just as liberty is real and indestructible, so freedom is innate in the mind. Man is born free. The children even of animals must seek to learn the true nature of the world or die. A baby begins to seek facts as soon as it can see, and nothing can blunt its curiosity but satisfaction; or disappoint its brain but lies and confusion.

18. Old writers who distinguished between liberty, as absence of restraint, and moral

freedom, as a positive and unique power, introduced a false division. Mind and body are one; and creative power belongs to the whole man. Just as moral judgment is the decision of a formed character, so freedom of mind is a quality of the whole character, and its action. The distinction between freedom in the mind, as the special quality of one free from prejudice or fear, and liberty only has value in so far as the action of thought differs from that of muscle. Thought cannot be seen, and therefore it cannot be directly judged or coerced. Despots can compel men's bodies, but their hold upon minds is indirect and uncertain.

To describe Socrates in gaol as a free-minded man without liberty does not mean that he had lost the natural creative power of his mind ; that power remained, and it has worked among humanity for more than two thousand years. It is only a way of saying that the freedom of Socrates' mind was beyond the power of the Athenian state which imprisoned and destroyed his body.

A millionaire who is stopped in a crowded pavement because he dare not walk under a ladder is a man with much liberty but small freedom of mind. His total power is great, but the power of his mind is limited.

But, in reality, this means that this total power,

his total liberty, is enormously weakened and restricted. For thoughts make deeds. The mind, therefore, is the heart of liberty, its last stronghold. It is because that stronghold is hidden and beyond the reach of any dictation that liberty grows irresistibly in strength. Modern organization requires educated men. The soldier and the worker are both in charge of elaborate machinery and they are obliged to use their wits. But trained minds cannot be prevented from thinking at large. They do not use their new power only to work a machine.

19. Education is therefore the key of liberty.* This was not seen by the old writers.† Even Mill begins with the grown men and says of children that they have no right to liberty. But it is seen by the modern dictators, whose argument is this : "Liberty is to do what a man likes. Therefore, if we teach him to do what we like, he will still have liberty. He will feel no restraint. He will be that most valuable slave who delights in his blind obedience."

20. This plan is not only in action, but millions believe that it is effective. Scientists speaking in the name of science and with all its prestige declare that it is justified by man's own

* *On Liberty* : J. S. Mill, 1859.
† They say, "The service of God is freedom" ; but they ought to say, "To serve freedom is to serve God."

nature—that he is a creature entirely determined or formed by external forces.

They talk of Pavlov and conditioned reflexes, or they declare that all conduct is due to glandular action and that a single injection can transform a man's character.

Millions who never heard of Pavlov or reflexes, and who have the vaguest notion of glands, still know that the old doctrine of man's essential responsibility is denied.

21. This belief, supported by many biologists and an immense mass of popular talk, is probably the most dangerous enemy to liberty and democracy now active. It is strong in the democratic countries, especially in America, because of the high prestige of science in all countries where minds are free.

Scientists, who are usually strong supporters of liberty, have been during the last sixty years among its worst enemies. For the dictators can find in their works not only good excuse but excellent support for abolishing liberty and freedom and science itself. They say, "Man is a mechanism, and all the evils of the world arise because he does not work properly or in accord with other mechanisms. We shall make him into a perfect machine and everybody will be happy."

If they are right, there is no case for

19

democracy, which ought to be and will be destroyed.

22. But they are not right and modern science does not support them even when it seems to do so. Scientists deal in abstractions. They are obliged to treat nature as a mechanism even though they assume that their own minds, which are part of nature, are not mechanical. Thus the same scientist who writes of a man's body as if it were a machine demands liberty for man to form his own opinions and to act upon them. Machines do not study science. A motor car or a typewriter has no opinions and no creative liberty. What is more, those scientists who study differences in bodies and not their likeness point out that they inherit their differences and that each child is born with a nature and quality peculiar to itself.

This capacity may be injured or stunted by a bad education or illness, but it cannot be changed. For instance, a child who on account of illness suffers injury to the thyroid gland may seem dull-witted. Injection of thyroid extract may cure it and enable it to use its intelligence. Such a child is in exactly the same position as any sick person who is prevented by illness from using his natural powers. A clever man may be changed by a tumour of the brain into a maniac or an imbecile. An operation could restore him to health, but it could not change his essential powers.

23. The theory that men are machines is false and those who have advanced it contradict themselves, but many who take no account of theories believe that children can be trained to think and act alike.

They say, "No one wants to make natural engineers into clerks ; but it is conflict in religion and politics which produces civil war and revolution, and this conflict can be easily avoided by teaching children the same religious and political creed. We may differ from the dictators about the value of the creed they teach, but uniform creeds can and should be taught. They have been taught with great success."

They point for example to the Catholic church, the Buddhist and Mahometan churches, to the political dogmatic training in the nazi, fascist, and other nationalist parties.

24. Uniformity in any religious or party order existing to-day is due not to mass education but selection. A church or party is not a people but certain members of the people who join together because they think and feel alike. Priests are supposed to have a vocation. The churches and dogmatic political parties, like the nazi and the communist, are all minorities

in the nation. They are not formed by a mass education, but they choose a common education because they are already similar in tastes and opinion. Such active priesthoods and party members must be sharply divided from the numbers who profess the dogmatic religion or party faith. We see photographs of fascist children parading with arms. These are true objects of mass education, because they are not selected.

25. It is obvious that mass education in opinion, like all education, has effect on children. Such mass education has existed for centuries among primitive African tribes and in certain countries under priestly or caste rule. Buddhist, Hindu, or negro children are all taught the same religious ideas, which are usually also political. This traditional teaching has not been planned by any dictator, but it is the best possible test of the whole modern theory of mass political education, because it has been practised for long enough to show its effects.

These are two. Where it succeeds in obtaining uniformity or any high degree of uniformity, it produces stagnation and political weakness. It destroys all initiative, all progress even in the arts, and makes great races the easy prey of foreign conquerors. A pattern authoritarian education almost ruined even so great a civilization as the Chinese.

22

When it breaks down it leaves the people helpless to judge for themselves and to form their own opinions. They are ready to believe anything, to follow any spell-binder. This was one result of the breakdown of the mandarin system in China towards the end of the old empire. But the same confusion of mind and moral instability can be seen in any country among members of sects or parties whose creeds have been exploded.

26. Mass education always fails in countries when there is any critical tradition, any freedom. It is surprising how little freedom, how small an amount of independent thought, in comparatively few minds, can bring it to ruin. It is true to say that in a nation, as distinct from a church or a party, mass education is a hopeless enterprise unless the whole people is illiterate and isolated from the rest of the world. Nobody expected it to fail in Russia, but it has not avoided the bitterest conflict of opinion. The same conflicts exist in Germany and Italy.

But even the great churches of history, working with selected minds, cannot escape from plots and heresies. They remain uniform only by purges. Their tendency is always to break up.

27. Thus mass education, even when it is limited to forming a standard political or

religious mind, can succeed only among illiterate peasantry. It produces then stagnation.

With literate peoples who have some freedom of mind and critical judgment it produces only an appearance of uniformity. Peoples under terror may repeat the orthodox opinions, but they do not believe them. As the Italian traveller said when he was asked his politics, "In England I am a liberal ; in Italy I am a hypocrite."

Hypocrisy has always been the result of mass education whether by church or state, and it is the ruin of both. It is corruption in itself and it is the mask of the secret assassin.

28. If, therefore, any state should succeed by a standard education in forming mass opinion among its peoples, it would secure its own ruin by stultifying the whole race ; but if, as always happens among literate peoples, it only succeeds in stultifying its own party members and those who are too young or too stupid by nature to think for themselves, it damages itself in direct proportion with its expense of effort.

29. Man, therefore, is not only unique in the possession of a natural liberty and desire for truth, but in his separate character. All his teachers and his state can do is to enable him to make the best of it. They can give him the power to realize himself in his own unique

nature and they can stultify and deform it ; *
but they cannot change its essential quality.

Since education has this power to help or
cripple, it is the most important function of
society. It gives men the use of their own
liberty. A democratic theory of the state which
ignores education betrays liberty at its source.

30. Though men differ in character, their
difference is not so great as their likeness. All
over the world they seek similar ends. Every
democracy has similar objects : more liberty,
more leisure, more realization. There is thus
a common will of humanity which, since it is
the will of liberty, must realize itself.

Rousseau was right in seeing that this common
will tended to justice and peace. His mistake
was in a false definition of liberty, which obliged
him to invent the paradox of men at once free
from restraint and forced to obey a general will.
All governments impose restraint. A good
government is one which restrains a man for the
sake of his own liberty or the general liberty :
for justice, for peace, for instruction. A child
may be kept in school to learn the ABC, but
reading is a liberty, a power which it is society's
duty to give him. A man who can read has
more freedom than an illiterate.

31. A common will of the world exists.

* Para. 219 : Education for Liberty.

It is not, as Rousseau supposed, a general will which is always right because it is impartial. It is the common desire of the majority of people, throughout the world, for liberty, peace, security, and the reign of law. It arises from the likeness of men's minds and the liberty of their reason, which in the majority perceives everywhere that they gain more advantage, more power, and more happiness in peace and order than in war and disorder. They see that the liberty of the few to make war is the enemy of the many, who are better served by peace.

Their common will grows stronger with liberty, because the more liberty men have—the more security, the more pay, leisure, and the greater power of happiness—the more they have to lose by war or injustice.

Just as real democracy by mere persistence through countless generations invariably has its way within any nation, so the will and mind of the world democracies seeking international peace, justice, and security must finally have their way in the world.

CHAPTER III

Liberty, Historical

32. Liberty, because it is real, makes its own way in spite of theories. It grows like a tree, which is also part of real creation. During the nineteenth century, when all thinkers had the old and confused ideas of it, it actually overcame and defeated its own friends. This process is strange to watch.

33. Mill—whose great book on liberty, published in 1859, is, with Rousseau's *Social Contract*, one of the rare classics of political thought—had the abstract conception of liberty as absence of restraint. He was therefore forced to distinguish between public and private action. He imagined the state as keeping the ring in which men and minds, according to their private inclinations and characters, could fight their own battles. He laid down rules to stop encroachment by the state on the ring.

34. This led him directly to the contradiction of saying, first, that the danger of democracy was stupidity in its rulers,* and,

* As if a bad carpenter would do better work with blunt tools.

secondly, that the civil service ought not to be made attractive to clever men at the expense of private business.

Such contradiction is inevitable under the old idea and infects all the liberal thought of the past.

35. Thus Mill and Spencer,* and Gladstone himself, were suspicious of all state action. They looked upon it as an encroachment and restraint, and they could not solve the puzzle of legislation. When Mill and Gladstone demanded the extension of the franchise, they called it emancipation, the removal of a restraint. They could not explain, and it did not strike them to explain, how a vote could be a removal. They did not see that what the party had accomplished was a devolution of political power.

The vote, though it was really power, was not obviously restraint, so that it did not come into conflict with the ideas of the party. But the factory acts, forced through against strong opposition, laid obvious restraint upon employers.

Spencer, who had great influence throughout Europe and especially in Russia, bitterly opposed them. He wrote for fifty years to prove that the welfare of mankind, since it depended on the evolutionary process and the struggle for existence, required a complete absence of

* Herbert Spencer, 1820–1903, Victorian philosopher.

28

restraint. Thus he held sincerely that to restrict child employment was an outrage on liberty, that the sale of adulterated food or poison should not be checked, and that all post offices should be in private hands.

Good liberals were bound to agree with him that all restraint was an evil, but they continued to draw up acts of regulation. The liberty that they did not recognize, the power of the people and their own creative imagination, obliged them to do so.

36. All politics are real in this sense, that they deal with real people and their demands, with real situations, where there is suffering, ambition, passion, and anger ; and politicians, struggling from day to day with real problems, do not care for theories unless they can illustrate a speech. But ideas, though they work slowly, are always at work. Their power over a length of time is great, and the only counteraction is an idea equally strong and better founded. But since only one liberal theory * held the field, that state restriction was in itself bad, while the practical men, supposing themselves to hold that theory, continued to do what they perceived necessary from day to day, a deep

* *Man versus the State*, Spencer, 1884. He asks, "Is it not cruel to increase the sufferings of the better (*i.e.* by taxes) that the sufferings of the worse may be decreased ?"—income-tax 6*d.* !

division split the party and confused even its leaders.

37. These leaders, and especially the younger radicals, had seen that the devolution of political power did not by itself give justice or security to the people. The poor with votes were not much better off than the poor without votes. They therefore proposed to lighten poverty by state action, by pensions and insurance. They would tax the rich to help the poor.

This legislation, like the factory acts, was proposed in the name of justice. The radical leaders did not speak of liberty, but of the wrongs of the poor. But the idealists of the party, those who were able to take a wide view over the political field, could see that a complete revolution had taken place, that the whole idea underlying the philosophy of men like Mill and Spencer had been reversed, and that liberty, in the only conception they had of it, was not any longer the ruling principle of liberal government.

38. The Liberal Government of 1902–1914 is justly thought one of the greatest in British history. But its achievements were all in the teeth of the old theory that state regulation was the enemy of private liberty. That idea was now being criticized. Mr. Asquith, speaking in 1902, said that it was time to give more positive

aims to liberal policy. But the fundamental creed of liberals was still the same : that liberty was absence of restraint, and that state action was therefore an evil. Thus liberals were in the position of fighting state socialists for proposing exactly the same kind of legislation which their own government had started.

They had to attempt a demarcation of private interest and state interest ; and every day the lines shifted, but always in the same direction.

They did not see that the Asquith government had not diminished real liberty but enormously increased it, and that it could still be increased. The liberty of the subject is not coming to an end—it is beginning ; and the state is as necessary to it as subjects are necessary to the state. But it must be a state organized for the distribution as well as the increase of power, and not for its centralization ; that is, it must be a democratic state.

CHAPTER IV

Man and State. Which is Master?

39. The poor think of liberty almost entirely in terms of economic power, because money is the outer gateway to all satisfactions. A poor man cannot learn without money ; he cannot have games, music, art—any pleasure, from the worst to the best. He cannot realize himself. Nevertheless, economic power is subject to limitation and the pleasure is not. That is to say, some powers are of necessity limited, and others, like the power of enjoyment taken by itself, are not limited.

Political and economic liberty are both limited by their nature, because there is only a certain quantity available for distribution.

A man wants time, as well as liberty, to enjoy himself. But leisure is at the expense of production. The man as producer of wealth is in conflict with himself as a user of it ; or, to put it more clearly, the worker must choose at a certain point between wealth and leisure. He will, of course, strike a balance. He will say,

"If I can only make more money by giving up so much leisure, I will keep the leisure."

This balance marks one of the external limits of economic power. Others are natural limits, such as the limitation of ground available for use ; or necessary limits, like the rights of others.

Powers of enjoyment, on the other hand, have no necessary limits. Thus, men spending the same amount of money on a race meeting, a dinner, a play, a concert will have entirely different amounts of enjoyment, and there is no connection or balance between them. There is no limit to pleasure and also it is not divisible. It increases by sharing. Yet these powers are given by society in education, and in all its acts designed for public security, order, and amusement.

40. At first sight powers of enjoyment, contemplation, and love do not seem to belong to the same category as political and economic power. Can we think of enjoyment as a use of liberty in the same sense as voting, even though both are secured by the state ? An actual man, not the abstract political economic man, does not divide his activity into departments and say, "I have political liberty to vote this afternoon and to-morrow I am at liberty to take a holiday or to tell the manager what I think of him." He does what he wants to do. In the same way, a

man of musical taste going to a concert does not say, "I owe all this to the liberties seized and defended by my ancestors ; my education, my power to go to concerts at all, the public order which enables concerts to be given and the industry which enables them to be paid for." He simply goes to the concert and enjoys it. He accepts, like most people, the enormous benefits of organized and distributed power as if they were as natural to humanity as air.

41. The powers of imagination and enjoyment are not limited by necessity ; political and economic powers are limited. Men seeking these powers are in open competition. This necessary conflict is often represented as the root fact of history and the source of government. The suggestion is that men, in their natural wild state, co-operate in love or friendship and do not need government ; but so soon as they seek power over one another or exclusive possession of property, they come into conflict. This conflict continues, making them all wretched, until one conquers all the rest or until they agree to appoint a ruler enforcing laws upon all equally. In both cases, government has arrived.

This is fanciful both in history and psychology. It has importance only because it still forms the root idea of much political thought. Many say, "Let us abolish the struggle for political and economic power by an equal distribution of wealth and votes, and government will be no more needed."

42. But this is an abstract idea. It takes no account of the real nature of man, nor even of liberty itself, in whose name it speaks. Man is not a political or economic animal. He is moved by sympathies, tastes, faiths which have nothing to do with politics or cash, and he is always ready to fight for them. Religious wars, nationalist wars, what are now called wars of ideology are neither economic nor political, but ideal. They seek power to impose a rule of life not only upon the political and economic system of a people, but its thoughts, pleasures, its total being. What is more, this struggle, open or tacit, carried on by violence or by argument, is the perpetual condition of all societies. There is no man who does not wish to find others in agreement with him, and many of the chief pleasures in life, even in the arts, are dependent on a consensus of taste. Plays are not acted, music not performed, books not published unless there is a certain minimum number of people ready to enjoy them.

But the final source of conflict and of the instability which belongs to all institutions is in the nature of liberty itself.

43. Since man is creative, he produces continually a new situation, not only in the arts and sciences but in politics and industry. Every invention changes the economic balance and so has its effect in politics. A new political idea or movement always has economic and social consequences. In the real world it means a change in power or status, wages and comfort for a certain number of people. But, as creation never stops, there is a never-ending process of adjustment. It is because a modern democratic society possesses much liberty, and therefore much creative power, that it appears more unstable, more full of conflict and confusion than any yet seen.

This tumult of life is the health of society. There is no more reason to be troubled by it than by the noise and inventiveness of a healthy child. It is not a sign of degeneration but of growing power. It does not argue for repression of liberty, but its protection. It makes government a necessity, not only to keep the peace but to adjust the claims of different creeds and ideas, each seeking dominion. Anyone who knows the history of the English education acts understands this function of government. Some supreme authority is necessary in every state not merely for repression or organization, but for adjustment of novelty and solution of conflict.

44. The government in any state is distinct from its subjects, and this is true not only of monarchies and empires but democracies. A London constable acts with the same authority as a policeman in Berlin, and those who obey him do not suppose that they are giving themselves the order. The idea of self-government is a paradox which is contradicted in everyone's experience, for even a man who willingly obeys a law knows that he obeys an external authority. He does not command himself.

Democracy is not self-government, even in theory, but the rulership of the majority. In practice it is the rule of delegates who, being in office, are for the time in absolute command over the whole people. The difference between an autocracy and a democracy is in the attitude of people towards authority and their power to change it or modify it ; not in the nature of authority.

45. In history there has been a continuous modification of government—in democracies by political conflicts, strikes ; in autarchies by plotting and revolutions. Since man is creative in himself and dependent on society for the means of creation, he is always in private or open conflict with the government.

He rebels in his heart against any authority, but he asks, at least in his heart, for justice and opportunity, which only authority can secure to him.

Men have always said, "What is liberty if we can't do what we like? The state is our creation. Why should we obey it when it tyrannizes over us?" The state has always answered by sending its police. It says to rebels, "You owe everything to state protection and contrivance—your education, your security. It is in your own interest that I command you."

46. This conflict is universal and it has lasted from pre-history. Which ought to be master, man or state? If the question is put so, it has no answer. But answers have been made of four different kinds.

    (1) If man owes all to the state, the state has absolute right over him. This is the answer made by Plato, Hobbes, Hegel, Bosanquet in England, and the modern nazi philosophers.

    (2) If the state owes its reality and existence to men, man is absolute against the state and can refuse obedience to it when he chooses. This is the answer made by Bakunin and all anarchists.

    (3) Those which say both are master; Rousseau's view.

    (4) Those which say neither is or can be master, for all are at the mercy of

forces which man does not control. Spencer and the biological school, Marx and the Spenglerian school give this answer.

This last group seems to answer the problem by abolishing it. But the real problem is not abolished. Real men feel and hate the compulsion of states and fight against it every day ; and states find themselves checked even in their best intentions for men by rebellion, strikes, sabotage, and indifference. It was and is a real problem of suffering, struggling people and anxious governments.

47. Plato wrote the *Republic* when Athens had brought destruction upon herself. Demagogues had ruined the state by their reckless vanity and arrogance. He, therefore, imagined a state governed by wise men for good ends.

Plato says, in effect, that men are weak and foolish and unfit to know what is good without education. A good education takes many years. All cannot have it, but without it no one is fit to govern. Therefore governors must be a special class, and in order to rule well they must be absolute.

What is the object which Plato's absolute state was to achieve ? The realization of the good, which was to be discovered by the dialectic or logical inquiries of the wise men into the forms or universals : that is, goodness, beauty, truth. Thus Plato imagined a fixed and immutable scheme by which things and men ought to be governed, and it might be said that he did not make the state absolute, but the good.

Political theory deals with complex matters and uses uncertain language ; the best way of finding out what any political thinker really means is to look at his conclusions. What kind of state does he want, and why ?

Plato's state is absolute, it is repressive, it imposes strict censorship on the arts, and its rulers judge what is good not by asking what is good for men, but simply, what is good. It treats men as means to an end, and this end is ascertained by the rulers' insight. Moreover, this good is imagined by Plato as a fixed and complete scheme.

48. This idea of a fixed scheme for the world does not in itself exclude liberty. For a church or a state may hold that liberty for man is itself part of the final nature of things, willed by God, or independent of him.

So that both can say, like Plato, government must seek the highest good of its citizens, and yet, unlike Plato, permit liberty as part of that good.

But even the Christian Churches who do believe that God has given freedom to men are always tempted, in practice, to take away the freedom. For they think that God's scheme is complete and that they know it ; and so they are naturally impatient of contradiction, and tend to regulate the least details of man's life.

Plato had this conception more strongly almost than any other philosopher. For him, the whole scheme of things was immutable.

Liberty therefore, as creative power, had no place in his state. He did not even, like the Christian Churches, imagine liberty for man as part of God's plan. He did not conceive the idea of a creative force anywhere in real being.

Also, since he imagined the form or idea of the good as given immediately to his rulers by a kind of mystical insight, in practice he sought it in his own mind.

The books of the *Republic* are full of discussion about the nature of government, of art, of education ; in all of them we know that the conclusion is already formed. Plato is already convinced of the truth. He knows it in his mind, by insight. In the last resort, Plato's guardian philosophers are simply himself and the idea of the good is Plato's idea of the good. He belongs to the great class of religious and political theorists who have said in all ages, "I know inside me what is good for men, and they must do it."

49. Plato made the state master because he had known the miserable failure of a democracy, but he tried to make sure that his state master would be disinterested and benevolent. Plato's ideal republic has always been admired by philosophers * because their feelings are like his ; they hate disorder, folly, vanity, violence, falsehood, insecurity, and ugliness. All these things exist in absolute states as well as in democratic, and in the former there are evils which are worse than these because incurable : lassitude, cynicism, and indifference.

50. Hobbes, most logical founder of English political theory, wrote his book *Leviathan* during the Civil War of 1642–1648, at a time when Europe was torn to pieces by religious wars, when towns were destroyed every day and the people murdered, raped, and tortured by the hundred thousand in the name of Christianity. He considered that man left to himself always tumbled into misery. Man's natural state was war ; his chief passions were vanity and fear. But vanity operates chiefly in a democracy, where all men compete for power and distinction by lies or treachery ; whereas fear works upon the lonely monarch in his privacy. He is set above vanity and competition, but he can still fear. There-

* Ruskin was a modern Platonic. He writes, "How false is the conception, how frantic the pursuit, of that treacherous phantom which men call Liberty" : *Seven Lamps of Architecture*, Chap. VII.

fore, as absolute master, he will rule with precaution and foresight. He will be a good ruler.

Hobbes was one of those who grounded his theory of the state upon the idea of a social contract. This was a popular notion in the times when men were wont to appeal, in their conflicts, to a written authority, either legal or religious, and words like contract by themselves carried authority. Hobbes's conception of it was this : that men, finding their natural powers useless to them in a state of nature, which was war, handed them over by contract to the sovereign, who could then say, "I am not only your real but your legal master."

Hobbes, like Plato, derived his theory from introspection. He described man as he felt him to be, and he used his reason to justify the kind of state in which he himself could feel security.

51. Hegel, greatest of those philosophers who make states absolute, lived from 1770 to 1831, when nationalism was winning its first great conquests. His ideas still inspire not only German politicians but vast numbers in all countries who never heard of him. To understand them is to understand the political landscape everywhere, with its cliffs, thickets, and mud-holes.

43

For Hegel, the most important thing in the world is thinking. "Men," he says, "follow their ideas. Ideas guide men. Ideas make history."

Any man who has designed and made a house sees his idea, a new thought, turned into something real, an actual house, which goes on existing after he is dead.

52. So ideas make everything. What of man ? He can only be the idea of some greater mind—God's mind, or, as Hegel puts it, absolute mind ; a mind not dependent on any other. God's mind has therefore created all ideas, including man and states.

53. Hegel's idealist system is called dialectic idealism because he thought that absolute mind formed its ideas by a kind of argument within itself.

This dialectic process, for Hegel, explains all history, morals, science, art. For instance, the family, as a spiritual unity, generates as its opposite, the individual, selfish and isolated. But individuals soon find that, for their own benefit, they must help each other. So the idea of the state reveals itself in actuality, the ethical unity of individuals.

Family or private life as thesis splits into selfish individuals as antithesis, who come together again at a higher stage of ethical being, richer than any family life, in state or public life ; and the idea, present to each, of national unity and national service.

54. The dialectic is artificial and abstract. It does not square with the facts of history or psychology. It has never succeeded in telling us, as it should, what is going to happen next in the process of history. It does not even reveal the process of thought. A man may think by jumping from an idea to the opposite, or he may not. He may fly off at a tangent.

55. The argument of idealists from man's mind to God's mind is familiar. Mankind has always felt the unique quality of its own powers, and postulated a father or absolute god to explain them. The primitive savage made him a savage tyrant ; a modern physicist finds that he must be a mathematical physicist. No one, probably, can avoid a similar belief ; if not in God, in some alias for God, such as life force or mind or evolution.

56. The vital question is not, Does some power, mind, or God rule the world ? but, How does it rule ? Absolutely, or only by advice, persuasion ?

In the first case, liberty is an illusion ; in the second, it is real.

57. Those who believe in a life force or evolution are in the same position. Believers in a life force tend to doubt liberty. They need

not do so. For the life force may also be regarded as persuasive rather than compelling. It urges both sexes to marry and beget children. But many refuse to obey.

58. The question is confused by popular speech and religious use. "Hangs my helpless soul on thee" is poetry expressing an emotion. But it may become a doctrine expressing a creed. It then denies freedom.

The dividing line is, in practice, narrow. Hegel and Rousseau both began as rebels, believers in freedom. Both believed in a general will. But they ended in opposite camps, because for Hegel the general will was the absolute, realizing itself through men ; for Rousseau, man realizing himself through the collective will.

59. All monists and idealists who start by thinking of the world as a unity are tempted to deny real liberty to man. It is impossible for them to keep firm hold of the individual. Take the passage from Hegel :

"As a single individual . . . exclusive against other like individuals. In their mutual relations, waywardness and chance have a place ; for each person in the aggregate is autonomous." *

In this passage Hegel is writing not of men but nations ; and on the next page we find :

* Hegel : *Philosophy of Mind*, p. 545. Translated by W. Wallace. Clarendon Press, Oxford.

"As the mind of a special nation is actual, it admits the influence of geographical and climatic qualities. It is in time. But as a restricted mind its independence is secondary. It passes into universal world history. . . . This movement is the path of liberation for the spiritual substance . . . it is the revelation to the outward eye of a universal spirit, a world mind."

That is to say, Hegel, beginning with the idea of a world mind, including all subordinate minds, naturally thought of nations as subordinate individual minds. For, if man's mind is simply a bit of God's mind, any part of universal mind can be described as an individual : for instance, that of a club. A bridge four would answer most of Hegel's requirements for a nation : a collective will to act together ; a common law ; and a common purpose. An Hegelian would describe the common will of a bridge four as a real will, and by real he would mean having actual authority over each member of the four and an independent existence.

This, then, is the crux. Is the national will real, as a man's will is real, and does it rule absolutely and directly ? Is it, as Hegel writes, "a self-possessed, self-realizing reason," to which absolute obedience is due because it is God's ? *

* *Philosophy of Mind*, p. 160. Wallace's translation.

60. Hegel's theory of the state as God's will in the world may seem absurd, but it is not so. It arises psychologically, like Plato's contempt for democratic folly and weakness, from actual experience in the real world. Hegel saw the collapse of the old German empire, by its own internal disunity and incompetence, and suffered by it. His own house and belongings were looted by Napoleon's soldiers after Jena. He saw all about him good, wise, and brave men utterly helpless, by themselves, even to defend their own homes and their own honour against organized armies whose only objects were loot and glory.

All idealist and absolutist theory is rooted in this truth, that man by himself is weak and dependent.

61. Hegel's state-theory had immense power in the last century. It was logical, it fitted together, it applied to facts ; the supporters of liberty, even Mill, had nothing to bring against it except moral feelings or scattered epigrams which often marched against each other. Liberty had no case. Political thinkers like Carlyle, writing in the first half of the century, and Bosanquet, writing in the second, could not find a good word for it.

62. All who come under Hegelian influence must despise democracy. But it must not be

thought that they do so out of blindness or
stupidity. They see both sides of the case.
Here is Professor Troeltsch speaking just after
the war in Berlin :

"Germans have different ideas from those of
Western Europe and America—they are based
on the idea of the romantic counter-revolution.
They created the organic idea of the group
mind, instinct with anti-bourgeois idealism." *

Thus Troeltsch, like Hegel, says that the state
should be master, because it is a real thing,
greater than people, a group mind which lives
and feels, and realizes itself in the process.

Troeltsch writes in a later work :

"Those who believe in an external and divine
law of nature, the equality of man, and a sense
of unity pervading mankind cannot but regard
the German doctrine as an odd mixture of
mysticism and brutality. Those who take the
opposite view . . . are bound to consider the
West European world of ideas as a world of cold
rationalism and equalitarian atomism, a world
of superficiality and pharisaism."

Thus for Troeltsch, as for all absolutists,
church or state, a democracy is the rule, or
rather the anarchy, of selfishness, where men

* From an address delivered in 1922 to the German Hochschule
für Politik. See Appendix, *Natural Law and the Theory of Society*,
by Otto Gierke, trans. by Ernest Barker. Camb. Univ. Press, 1934.
The introduction by Professor Barker gives an excellent analysis of the
idea of group personality.

struggle like maggots for their share of a decaying society ; where only riches have honour and the artist or man of learning is regarded with pity and contempt.

Troeltsch was not an isolationist. He pointed out that the nationalist theory of the group soul ought to be part of the world theory of a world soul. He supported the League of Nations. Nevertheless his ultimate belief is that the spirit of a nation is a real thing which must be absolute against its members, for otherwise neither a nation nor its people can have a real spiritual life.

63. Many will say : National spirit does exist ; it is real because it is effective. Men die for the nation.

The truth is that the words real and spirit are ambiguous. An idea does not really exist. A man may plan a house, but if he dies before he builds it, there is no house. The idea has not been made real. The word spirit in the dictionary means two things : intelligent or immaterial part of man, soul ; and moral condition or attitude, mood. Thus we say : Man has a rational spirit ; or we say : He spoke in a spirit of forgiveness.

These meanings appear different. In the first case we mean : Man has a characteristic described as spiritual. In the second case we mean simply : This specific man acted in a certain manner. When we say the spirit of Christ, we mean not only the character of Christ but something that remains in the world, so that it can be said of a man, "He acted in a Christian spirit." But to act in Christ's spirit is to act in a manner characteristic of Christ. So that the two meanings of spirit have a common root in the conception of something characteristic.

When people talk of the British spirit, they mean something characteristic of the British people. The German Volksgeist is the German character. When Germans obey the Volksgeist, the German spirit, they act in a manner which they conceive to be characteristic of Germans. But where does this character or spirit reside ? Does it exist independently of living people ?

64. Hegel, Gierke, Bosanquet * say yes, and many English, Irish, and American people, though perhaps they have not thought about the matter, act and speak in the same way. They do so because they feel that the nation is something not only superior to individuals but essentially different from them : a real independent existence. But national spirit is an ideal, and ideas are not real.

The spirit of a team is different from that of

* Bernard Bosanquet, 1848–1923 : *The Philosophical Theory of the State.*

its separate members. They do not possess it except when they act as a team. But it is not a real thing, living in the pavilion and issuing mysterious orders. It is a tradition, a sentiment, or idea embodied in words and passed from one individual to another.

Tradition, patriotism, the ideas of national honour have immense power ; so also do ideas common to humanity—brotherhood, equality ; but they are real only in the acts of individual men.

65. The confounding of ideal existence with the real, common in idealist philosophy, has other bad consequences as well as absolute state theory. For a man who thinks that the world is nothing but ideas is very apt to conclude that his ideas can make facts to suit himself.

Hegel, of course, saw the conflict between ideal and real, will and fact. He saw that there was something in the world intractable by any man's mind. His whole system was meant to explain that this dualism which puzzled other thinkers was a necessary one.

66. But Hegel's model of the world was not being limited by its own reality, as a man's ambitions are limited by his physical existence, but a self-conscious mind producing the real out of itself. Therefore his reality was depen-

dent on an idea in a mind ; it had no firm being of its own.

Moreover, this mind in practice was Hegel's mind.   What other mind could he know ?

67. Hegel's successors, modern philosophers of the national soul, write so :

"The first note which sounds to me as warning 'Guard yourself against all things not of Nordic origin, as being un-German and therefore objectionable.'

"Since German Socialism is National Socialism, it is wholly a question for the statesmen, whose duty it is to direct the play of ideas and thereby make history."

These are extracts from Professor Werner Sombart.*   They show the inevitable end of all state theory which stands upon the reality of a group soul or national spirit.

68. In sum, the flaw in Hegelian philosophy is its failure to establish a reality over against mind.   For, to an Hegelian, external reality includes other men.   Therefore he denies the reality, liberty, and independence of other men. The Hegelian system, like all idealist systems, is egocentric.   The flaw in Hegelian state theory is not in its emphasis on national spirit but in making this spirit independent of living minds and their critical reason.

* *Deutscher Sozialismus*, Werner Sombart.   Translation for Princeton University Press, 1937.

69. The Volksgeist, the spirit of a nation, is merely the character and tradition of a nation, to be studied and criticized like any others. To make a separate being of it is to put upon a throne the most foolish and hollow idol yet seen in the world and to submit to the rule of any mystical fanatic who chooses to interpret its will.

Hegel's answer to the problem is, therefore : The nation is master and the nation is God.

70. The next class solve the problem by saying, "Man is absolute. He alone can know what is best for himself. He must therefore be free of all government."

Pure anarchist theory is rare. For it is hard to conceive of man independent of social relations. Most anarchists therefore assume that human nature, left to itself, is not only good and wise, but concordant in action. They ground their theory in a law of nature acting through men.

The idea derives from the Stoics, who believed in a *jus naturale*. They said, "Man has from nature a law superior to those of any state." Stoic theory actually modified Roman law.

71. The chief systematic anarchists all belong to the nineteenth century. Proudhon, 1809–1865, invented the name anarchy. He believed that :

"There exists a natural system of social economy which men realize day by day and which I propose to lay bare."

Proudhon opposed violence. He thought that education and organization of the workers, certain economic reforms, and, above all, the final revelation of the natural laws innate in human affairs would transform society. He writes :

"Je veux seulement montrer que la société comme la nature est soumise à des lois éternelles et immuables . . . qui ne changent pas selon la caprice des hommes." *

Bakunin, 1814–1876, his chief disciple, was not so logical. He believed in the natural law, but preached violence. He hated all government and declared that even Comte's ideal government of reason would be "impotent, ridiculous, cruel. Only one government is possible. That of man by himself agreeing freely to obey natural laws." †

72. Kropotkin, a disciple of Tolstoy, believed that there is in nature an instinct for co-operation, even among animals. He denies that evolution is the result of competition, which degrades a species. To him the state is unnecessary.‡

* *De la creation de l'ordre dans l'humanité*, P. J. Proudhon.   Paris, 1843.
† *God and the State.*   Freedom Press, London, 1910.
‡ *Mutual Aid.*   Heinemann, 1904.

Kropotkin is, of course, right in saying that men help each other, that animals co-operate. But he simplifies too much. He notices the compassion of men, but not their natural pugnacity. Above all, he ignores the fact that primitive communities are not anarchic. They are closely governed by social and religious sanctions.

73. Tolstoy set God in the place of dialectic or natural law. He hated the state and described all government as violence :

"Evil-doers must not be punished, because all are equals and brothers. In the Christian life-conception alone every man is free, and it alone can give freedom from all human authority." *

Tolstoy, like Kropotkin, supported his case by special pleading. He writes of the New Testament, where it records the driving out of the money-changers : "This is not Christian." His argument is that Christ in using violence was not Christian.

But Tolstoy, like Proudhon, like a hundred anarchist thinkers from Shelley to the humble shoemaker Sacco, was a man of noble life and generous sympathy, who did magnificent service in the cause of liberty and justice. To the

* *The Kingdom of God is Within You.* Free Age Press. No rights reserved, undated. Bodleian stamp, 1904.

anarchists liberal thought and the cause of freedom owe much of their ideas and half their victories.

Anarchists, nevertheless, deny liberty. The power they set above individual man, whether they call it serial dialectic, natural law, or God, is absolute.   Moreover, in practice each of them —Proudhon, Bakunin, Kropotkin, Tolstoy—like Hegel, reads the will of this power in his own will.

74. Rousseau is unique in his solution, for he contrives that both man and state shall be absolute, thus.   Man has good will by nature. He is born free.   If a state truly represents him, it too will be good.   Let him by contract surrender his private will to the collective will, and it will govern him with his own good will.   He will remain free, and Rousseau has fulfilled his object, to discover a form of society such that "each uniting himself with all may still only obey himself and remain as free as before." *

This paradox may seem absurd, but Rousseau argues plausibly that men, outside their own personal interests, are impartial, and that in a general assembly the majority is therefore impartial.   Rousseau, in fact, holds that the general will is always right.   It may therefore force a man to obey it.   He makes the state

* *Du Contrat Social*, Chap. VI.   Longmans, Green, 1918.

57

supreme. But yet, since his ruling idea was man's absolute right to liberty, he begot both the Declaration of Independence in America, and of the Rights of Man in France. Two liberal revolutions sprang from Rousseau ; one counter-revolution in Germany ; and a double revolution in Russia, when a liberating movement passed into dictatorship.

Both sides, the Hegelian absolutists, the anarchists, have taken inspiration from him. He has not solved any problems, but increased them.

75. The fourth class say, "The conflict is illusory. Neither man nor state controls history." Two chief representatives are Herbert Spencer and Marx.

Herbert Spencer believed in an evolutionary process, and looked upon all state interference as wrong because it might prevent the working of this process by competition. He wished to abolish even the post office as a state service.

Spencer in practice is an anarchist. He says, "Leave all to the law of nature." He differs from Proudhon only in his notion of the law. Proudhon says, "Man is by nature co-operative and friendly." Spencer says, "Man is by nature competitive and jealous."

76. Marx also believed in an automatic process ; but he called it dialectic materialism.

He took Hegel's theory of the dialectic, but he said, "Conflict is not between ideas, but between economic systems." He argues so :

"The feudal system became out of date. Economic progress demanded a new kind of production. The serfs were turned off the land, which paid better under sheep. Wool workers were now wanted by capitalists for the new industry. The serfs became wage-earners.

"Feudal lord and capitalists both profited, but the former was now unnecessary. Therefore the process got rid of him. Capitalists, seeking cheap food for their cheap labour, abolished the corn laws and ruined the landed men.

"Capitalist and proletariat are left face to face. But the former in the ordinary process of business seeks to enlarge his capital and cheapen his labour costs. Thus he organizes a vast central power of capital and also ruins his own markets. For the people are too poor to buy his products."

Finally,

"the centralization of the means of production and the solidization of labour reach a point where they prove incompatible with their capitalist frame. This bursts asunder." *

* *Das Kapital.* Trans. by Eden and Cedar Paul. Everyman, p. 846. See the excellent introduction by G. D. H. Cole.

The expropriators, who themselves expropriated the feudal lords, are expropriated in their turn. To put this in dialectic form :

"Capitalism, rooted in wealth, generates its opposite the proletariat, or rootless poor. But in the same process it destroys its own markets. It collapses and leaves state capitalism, which is a synthesis of capitalist production and proletariat use."

Marx does not think of violent revolution as a step in the dialectic. It comes about only because the actual frame of society has failed to give way to the process. Revolution is the earthquake caused because the thrusting forces in the body of society have been prevented from gradual adjustment.

Marx's dialectic ends with the communist state producing wealth for all. But during the transition to this state, and while the proletariat are still in revolution, there will be need for a dictatorship.

Many would say, therefore, that Marx answers the problem by making the state supreme. In real politics that would be the consequence of his theory. But Marx differs profoundly from Hobbes because he believes that man should and could have liberty ; from Hegel and the German idealists because he looks beyond the national state to an international reign of peace and good will ; and from Rousseau in his realism. He does not say, "Both are absolute," which is nonsense ; he says, "The state, by a certain process at work in society, is ordained at a certain stage of that process to be supreme, but at the next stage it will wither."

But Marx's dialectic, like Hegel's, denies real liberty to man.

77. Plato contradicts Rousseau, and Spencer looks upon Hegel as the worst enemy of mankind. But in fact all their theories come to the same thing, egotism.

Rousseau, the individual egotist, refounded the absolute idea of the state : that is, the state as egotist. The revolutionary communist, asserting the rights of the ego against tyranny, sets up the dictatorship of the communist ego. The argument is this :

Man is by nature good and cannot do wrong. If he is allowed to make a state to suit himself, it will be a good state.

A good state cannot do wrong and therefore it has absolute power over individuals to compel them to do right ; or, as Rousseau puts it, to force them to be free.

So all individualist and anarchist state-theory ends in absolutism. For the moment any man, whether philosopher or saint, assumes that his conscience or mind is a final law, he must assume also an absolute nature or God inspiring him and therefore all others. Therefore the absolute master or God rules the world and no man has rights against it.

78. The same process begins at the other end with Hegel's absolute. For the absolute inspires the Hegelian and therefore he is absolute against the state. So, in practice, the nazi, trained in Hegelian tradition, rebels against the German state in the name of the national spirit. He says, "The German spirit which I love and serve is in me and I must obey it." So Hitler justified his destruction of the German republic.

All religions are defied by their own most ardent disciples, from Savonarola to Tolstoy. The egotism of churches saying "I am the voice of God" has been confronted by the egotism of mystics repeating the same creed : "I am the voice of God, and yours is false. I cannot obey you."

The argument in all these cases is this :

This state or church represents a holy will. I too, a member of this church or state, have the holy will within me. Therefore I can do that will for myself and the state is unnecessary ; or, in opposing me, evil.

Thus pure anarchist theory leads to absolutism ; and absolutism always leads to anarchy. The double action can be shown thus :

Absolute individual right derived from nature or supreme God } implies { a nature or supreme God with absolute rights over all individuals,

and produces the absolute state or church, organized egotism.

Supreme nature or supreme God. Ideal or material dialectic
Any automatic historical process. The infallible Bible. Volksgeist.   The British spirit.   Germania, Italia, Britannia, Hibernia, etc. } implies { individual right grounded in nature's or God's will for the individual. A fixed economic or historical function to which an individual has absolute right. Direct access of individual to God's will and therefore absolute authority in him. Right in all who share the spirit to say, "I act in the name of the Volksgeist, etc., and no one can gainsay my right,"

and leads to anarchy, disorganized egotism.

The absolutists like Hegel and anarchs like Bakunin sit in the same darkness and cannot decide which is gaoler and which gaoled.

CHAPTER V

Solution of Conflict.
Standards and Norms

79. A conflict between equal rights is irreconcilable, for what shall decide between them ? A man who appeals to his own will and mind for guidance acknowledges no other right. There is no hope for mankind as long as it takes egotism, under any name, for a law of conduct.

Conflicts of will can be solved only by an appeal to some independent judgment or standard. In practice critics of society have never said, "I am right because I think so," but always, "I am right because God or evolution tells me so." Tolstoy referred his case to Christianity ; Rousseau to nature ; Marx to the dialectic. But, in fact, these standards were their own feelings or assumptions. They were not true standards because they were not independent of Tolstoy, Rousseau, or Marx.

A true standard or norm must be independent of all personal opinion. Such norms are used every day. When men differ about horses, say Bois Roussel and Bend d'Or, which was the faster, they do not try to settle the matter by argument or a fight, they appeal to the records set down from the stop-watch.

80. Many political theorists have sought a norm to mediate between states and men. Catholic theologians set up Canon Law above rulers and subjects ; the Jesuit Suarez declared that any man could refuse obedience to his own state law when it was in conflict with Canon Law.

Locke, often called the father of English democracy, found his standard, or third thing, in natural law. He believed man had certain rights by nature, because God had created him independent and free ; and that therefore no one has the right to harm another in his life, health, liberty, or possessions.

Locke distinguished society from the state. Society was the body of free citizens enjoying by birth their natural rights ; as against the state, which was simply a governing body under contract with them to carry out certain duties considered useful and necessary, such as the collection of taxes and the administration of justice.

It could be changed at the will of society, and society had the right to change it, by rebellion, if it encroached upon natural rights.

Krabbe, Professor at Leyden, in his normative philosophy has looked for a norm in "the agreement or consonance of individual convictions of right." *

He means that men have a common sense of right and wrong. He writes : "The creative force of law is the conviction of people that its objects are right."

81. Obviously all these theories express some truth. The idea of natural law and rights is as old as the Stoics, and it represents a feeling common to men in all societies, the feeling natural to liberty seeking its own realization, that what is sauce for the goose is sauce for the gander. It may be restricted to one class or sex, but even a savage under patriarchal law feels injustice if his equal in age and rank receives special treatment. Children feel it strongly. Such a feeling is the root of the idea that law is a natural thing, part of the human mind.

It was because of this feeling based in actual psychology that the theory of natural law has had such a powerful effect in history—especially when, like Locke's version, it supports the individual against authority.

82. The theory of natural law and natural

* *Die Moderne Staatsidee.* Translated by Sabine and Shepard as *The Modern Idea of the State.* D. Appleton & Co., 1922.

rights is, of course, bound up with that of social contract.* All have the same basis in the actual life and thought of any community. The germ of all can be found in any nursery where one child says to another, "You've no right to touch my horse, I never take your engine."

83. The moral idea of reciprocal rights and duty is at work in all societies. It is one of those which inform liberty in its perpetual drive for realization. But the political theories founded upon it, such as those of natural right and social contract, have not given any permanent solution to social conflict. They can be used to support either the despot or the rebel, according to interpretation. A tyrant can say, "My right is divine" : that is, natural ; and so can any anarchist. The notion of contract can be interpreted by Hobbes to support an absolute monarchy, or by Locke to justify a revolution. For the terms of the imaginary contract are themselves a matter for imagination.

In the same way, Krabbe's norm would in practice be personal opinion. It appeals to an innate sense. It is subjective in its roots.

84. Many have found a standard in the moral consciousness. T. H. Green, 1836–1882,

* *The Social Contract*, Gough, Clarendon Press, 1936, is the best and latest authority.

an English idealist philosopher who had great influence on political ideas, thought, like Plato, of the good state as one realizing for men their highest moral development. He is impressed by the force of moral ideas, and he remarks that Napoleon, though seeking his own glory, had to pretend to relieve oppressed peoples : "So bad men are overruled for good."

Green's thought is really Platonic.* He imagines his ideal state as existing solely for the realization of good will in its members, and this good will is conceived in moral terms. In practice, Green's state would be little less repressive than Plato's ; but his lectures have the same kind of attraction as the *Republic*. He owes his influence to a fundamental truth in his creed, that everyone does use moral standards in judging the actions both of men and states.

It is impossible to make any judgment of right and wrong without assuming a fixed standard of moral law. Such judgments therefore do not arise spontaneously in the conscience or feelings ; they refer facts to an ideal standard, necessarily external to the judge, and grasped by reason.

Of course, many think that they are guided by conscience when they are really judging by

* See his *Lectures on the Principles of Political Obligation*. Longmans, Green, 1895.

ideas acquired in youth. They have only forgotten where their standards come from.

Moreover, moral judgment is not opinion ; it is tied to the facts. This was the flaw in Kant's notion of a man bound to tell the truth, even to a murderer who asks where his victim is hiding. To tell the truth in such a case would be a crime. A man has no right to conceive of himself as the machine tool of a principle ; he cannot get rid of the responsibility of moral freedom.* He must study the facts and use his invention to devise the right means of obtaining from them the highest possible good. A man who is convinced that war is evil may volunteer to fight against a bigger evil, such as the domination of injustice, cruelty, and violence in the world.

85. He knows his duty not by reference to some mysterious prompter, but to a moral standard ; to an idea of what the world ought to be. It is true that the characteristic which urges man to achieve this better world is innate and mysterious. But there is no doubt that he must use reason to achieve it.

86. Moral standards are the same everywhere. All people admire courage, generosity, unselfish devotion. But moral approval has

* *Theory of Good and Evil*, Rashdall, p. 175 ; Clarendon Press, 1924. *Principia Ethica*, Moore, p. 181 ; Camb. Univ. Press, 1903.

been given to the nazi revolution as well as the Spanish. It has been used to justify the shooting of communists in Spain as well as kulaks in Russia.

Of course, one can say, "The Russian revolution was justified and moral ; the nazi was immoral " ; but if anyone asks why, the only answer is, "Because it is obvious, because every decent person must think so." These are different ways of saying, "Because I feel it so."

It is an illusion that if all men were morally good, they would agree ; that the moral will can secure peace in the world. Moral leaders in every age have fought each other for men's souls.

Though moral values are constant in the idea, they no more provide a true standard for specific action than the æsthetic values colour, form, tone can give a permanent law by which critics can judge new works of art.

87. The ideal state, whether Plato's or Green's, existing only to realize the good, or the good will, is an abstract notion. It ignores the creative liberty of man which realizes the good, as well as evil, in an infinity of new forms.

88. Thus Locke's natural law, Green's moral will, Krabbe's sentiments of right are all subjective in origin. Even Canon Law arises, like Plato's *Republic*, from some man's *a priori* notions about

right and wrong. None of these are true norms because they are not independent of private judgment ; they are not standards of measurement.

89. The first attempt to find a true norm was made by Bentham in 1790.* He called it the principle of utility, which he defines as :

"That which approves or disapproves of every action according to the tendency which it appears to have to augment or diminish happiness. I say this of every action—and therefore not only of a private individual but of every means of government."

This norm came at once to be called "the greatest happiness of the greatest number." It will be seen that the standard of happiness was in fact a bad one, but it was a standard. It was a third thing set over against the confused action of states and men ; a measuring rod distinct from both. For the first time in history people could judge states and states could measure their own actions not by such varied and subjective terms as natural or unnatural, lawful or unlawful, but by objective facts. They could ask, "Is this or that act going to give happiness to the greatest number of people ?" This measure is still applied. It has soaked into the

* *Principles of Morals and Legislation*, by Jeremy Bentham, Chap. I. 1790.

common political thought of the world, of millions who never heard of Bentham, until, like the measure of time, it seems to them an idea of nature. They judge their own governments by it, their local councils, the whole apparatus of government and each other.

90. Bentham and his utilitarian school made a revolution within society which in a hundred years has transformed labour laws and municipal governments. The comparative peace of Britain during a long devolution of liberty was due almost entirely to the accident that a man of creative genius turned his mind to philosophy rather than religion, and in philosophy to political science rather than metaphysics.

An independent standard, even a doubtful standard like Bentham's utility principle, when it has been perceived by the people acts like a court of reference. It may be ignored for a time by one side or by both, but simply because it is always there, because, being an idea, it cannot be destroyed, it will be used at last. Each side will try to use it for its own purpose. But if it is a true norm it will prove inflexible.

91. Bentham's norm did not prove inflexible. The devolution of economic and political power was succeeded in 1870 by the devolution of intellectual liberty. The Liberal

72

Education Act proposed to make the people free, to give them the power to seek truth for themselves, and to enjoy for themselves the wealth of beauty and glory laid up in the nation's arts. The opposition was strong. Tory landowners and manufacturers joined with the Spencerian radicals to denounce an act which the first hated because it threatened their cheap labour market and the second because, according to their theory, it constrained liberty. This was a war of opinion. But now both sides appealed to Bentham's norm. The Gladstonians said, "We are giving happiness to the people." The tories answered, "What is the good of teaching children to read and write when already clerks are unemployed ? The country must have labourers and farm workers ; and there is not enough money to pay them high wages. To give them all education is to make them discontented with their lot and produce misery." They also pointed out that many of the people hated compulsory education and that the police had to enforce school attendance ; that parents looked upon the school board official as a petty tyrant.

92. The utilitarians argued that though education might cause discontent, it would in the end bring more happiness than pain. But, in fact, they had no case. What could they

say to such questions as these : "Which gives most happiness, whisky or music ?" "If Christ suffered more for unhappy men than Nero, was Nero a better citizen ?" "The Christians go to martyrdom, poets and artists starve rather than change their calling, learned men read themselves blind for learning, scientific men poison themselves in testing their drugs, nationalists throw away their lives for their countries, and all call themselves happy. What then is happiness and where is your measuring rod ?"

Everybody saw clearly that the measuring rod was not rigid, and that though men sought happiness, each man had a different idea of happiness ; that although governments could sometimes argue that they were aiming at the increase of happiness, often they aimed at something else. For instance, in the education acts they certainly aimed at something else. Yet they carried them, and the opposition soon agreed that they were right to do so.

93. People are now used to this idea that education ought to be given to children and that government ought to be responsible for giving it. If anyone said to them, "My little boy doesn't want to learn to read and so I'm not teaching him his letters," they would be shocked. But, in fact, it is an idea which flatly contradicts the old definition of liberty, the old ideas of

natural right and social contract, and the utilitarian doctrine of happiness. It says that government, whether legal government or the family government of parents, is right to force children to do what they don't like, not for their ultimate enjoyment but simply for their improvement in capacity and power.

But exactly the same process secured in former times first political liberty and then economic liberty. Each time the people demanded power and a certain section of the ruling class afterwards approved that demand, and raised it into a special right.

94. Green would say that these powers are in fact rights under the moral law. Most people would agree with him. The objection to idealist and Platonic theory is not that it uses moral standards—everyone does so—but that it gives no clue to the solution of moral conflict and that it sometimes denies liberty. For instance, a modern idealist might be inclined to say that education, a vote, and a fair wage complete the rights of men in society. But for all we know liberty, in its natural development, may make further and greater demands on the state.* How, then, is government to decide whether these demands are justified ? To what

* For instance, for national parks, national theatres in the provinces, etc.

standard can it appeal ? Not to the moral conscience, for that does not at present give any judgment on the matter, and if it did, would probably contradict itself.

95. Bentham's norm does not apply. But there is a norm which would, in the past, have applied to all three conflicts—for votes, for education, for economic power—a norm of liberty : the greatest liberty ; that is, the greatest power of mind and body to the greatest number.

Such a norm stands against the man so : How far has he realized his native powers ? And against a state : How far has it enabled men to realize their powers ? And it is independent of opinion. It should be noticed that the word liberty in this norm means true liberty— power, natural in man, collective in the state. For such a liberty involves, both in theory and practice, organic co-operation between man and state.

It is not therefore, like the old theories or even Bentham's norm, anarchic or disruptive. It does not set man against state or state against man. It implies a state organized to give power to man. But since states are made of men, the state that gives power gets strength. On the other hand, the state made of free men encroaches upon liberty at its peril.

96. The greatest liberty, or free power, of the greatest number is a third thing as distinct from men and states as mathematics. Economic power and standards of education are assessed in a thousand year-books. Hours of work and of leisure, even the conditions of work, of environment, and the opportunities of leisure, are all open to judgment by comparison.

97. Some might be shocked by this idea, that liberty has anything to do with cash. A hundred good sentiments declare that the poorest man with liberty is still a king.

In a real sense, apart from all sentiments, every man, however poor, has more than king-ship in him. He has the mark of the god, the power of the creator.

But, as we saw, one of the means by which that power realizes its own will is and must be economic. Education itself costs money ; and travel, which is a part of general education, costs the labour and contrivance and invention of others, expressed in money. Therefore a standard of liberty is not complete without a factor expressed as wage rates/cost of living.

This means that a poor country cannot have so much liberty as a rich one. Sentimentalists may not like this conclusion, but they ought to notice that poor countries are all eager to get rich. They are seeking as much liberty as they can get.

I do not mean that money alone is the measure of liberty. Many of the finest and greatest men of the world have been poor. But for the mass of men, with which alone a standard can deal, poverty is a direct restraint on liberty.

Even among men born with such power that they easily excel the richest with all their opportunities, poverty is a restraint felt more bitterly than limitation of mind. A genius like Burns would not have changed his imagination, his essential liberty of mind, with any millionaire ; but poverty bore him down and killed him.

Travellers often admire what they take for liberty among peasants, and this may be a liberty of thought and political independence. But it is more usually a short range of idea. The poor are apt to be content with a narrow life. Many people see in this contentment the secret of happiness and a world's peace. The idea of it, born in the cottage visits of men like Rousseau and Kropotkin, sympathetic and despairing in a confusion to which they had no key, was the source of anarchist theories. But even Rousseau saw that it was not a stable condition.

In fact, those who argue that any contentment arising from limitation is a good one are supporting the dictators who say, "I will make the people like what suits my policy." They are also, as both Kant and Rousseau perceived, proposing an impossibility. Man refuses to be limited.

The liberty of the poor may seem like the liberty of the wise men who, having power for all achievements and triumphs, find their greatest pleasure in the simplest things, in a field's beauty, the love of children, and occupation without glory ; but it is as different as the trance of sickness from the peace of health. The poor man does not know, perhaps, what his want has taken from him, but neither do the blind and the deaf. Poverty is neither simplicity nor liberty. It is a prison. Caged birds are happy in themselves and an ornament in any drawing-room, but human creatures are not made for cages nor for the amusement of tourists.

98. Nations, classes, and districts are already compared by the standards of wages, education, housing, leisure ; and governments are judged by them. It only needs to be seen that these real standards, in practical use and rapidly extending in use throughout the world, are parts of a norm of real liberty.

That norm is complex. There are crossdivisions in the ordinary standards used in government publications. A small country like Denmark may have higher education but lower rates of pay than some of the United States.

An index norm for liberty, like the cost-of-living index, would include different factors. But though people have different tastes in food, though one man can live and be content on a regimen which would starve another, the cost-of-living index has been of immense value as a norm. It has given a fixed standard of measurement in thousands of political inquiries and discussions, in thousands of wage disputes which would otherwise revolve in the air. It provides the framework of comparison for new norms and new assessments of man's needs.

For though it is an arbitrary figure, it is bound to facts by a constant relation. When they change, it changes, and no man can alter it by an effort of will to suit his own moral or political prejudice.

This is the function of all scientific measurements, from the standard foot and pound at the Board of Trade to clock time and the artificial structure of mathematics.* All science stands on measurement, and until measurements and classifications were devised it existed only as single glances at a fact and isolated strokes of

* Standards of the international metric system are kept at Sèvres on ground controlled by an international committee.

imagination. It was in the condition of liberty at this moment, a thing as natural to man as knowledge, but unorganized, unclassified, misunderstood and confused ; so that men and parties, each serving liberty, yet fight against each other more violently than those who care nothing for liberty under any name.

Mexico and Uruguay might quarrel with the details of a normal standard accepted for Europe and the different states of the U.S.A., but unless they claimed that illiteracy and low wages were themselves virtues in a nation, they would still be dealing with a true norm and not with opinion.

99. The basic figure in a standard of liberty must stand for political liberty and freedom. For though real liberty belongs to all manpower, so that a high standard of living and education in any nation will automatically produce democratic power in that nation, it does so indirectly and obscurely. Since the nature of liberty is not exactly perceived, its workings can be misunderstood both by rulers and ruled.* Neither see where real power lies until in some crisis the people are found dominant.

In this manner, democracy has grown in

* The term "people" in all these contexts includes for democracies the whole of a nation and for the autarchies all but state servants.

obscurity, and emerged in all nations. In France and England it appeared by a regular and slow growth, so that from one year to another the difference has not been perceptible ; but in even any twenty years it has been great. In all the western monarchies with popular education, in Denmark, Sweden, Holland, Belgium, it has increased in the same manner ; in Germany and the old Austrian empire it was revealed suddenly by the collapse of the old governments.

But in both these latter cases it came into political power without political experience. Wherever a real democracy becomes actual by the collapse of an autocracy, wherever men whose power has been economic and industrial are suddenly obliged to assume political power also, they are bound to make mistakes. This is true even when the democracy, as in Germany and Austria, possessed a very large share of the intellectual power in the nation—of professional men, of the managing, directing, and scientific brains. Clever and even wise men with no experience of real power are apt to misuse it. They are too inflexible and rule by rote or by abstract theory, so that their firmness becomes despotism and their benevolence weakness.

100. Political experience under an autarchy with parliamentary forms is not experience of real political power. The result, as we have

seen, is that democracy, brought suddenly into actual political power, is apt to break down and lose that power. Moreover, it may also lose some of its essential power at the same time—its economic and educational liberty— and be driven to a relatively lower strength.

101. Assessment of political liberty may seem difficult to the layman. How should one assess the relative political power of a fascist, who votes for the corporation ; a nazi, who votes only for the Führer ; an illiterate Mexican, who has the full political right to vote for any-body, but must vote for the party ; and a western European. Even in actual democracies the value of the vote differs with the constitution.

There is no exact comparison, and none is needed, because political power alone is abstract. If the Mexican were not illiterate, his vote would be more effective ; if he also had high industrial or agricultural skill, his total power would be more formidable to others and more valuable to himself. Thus if a single basic figure were taken for an effective vote, it would still be expressive in a total figure, because it would be corrected by the other factors.

102. The factor for political liberty must be a high one relative to the whole index. Other-wise an autarchy with a high standard of educa-tion and living might make a better appearance

than a democracy. Many people would claim that this would be right : that the actual liberty of a professional man, with a wide education and a good income, in Germany or Italy, is greater than that of a country doctor in the back parts of the Midlands or Louisiana. But I would not agree. For political liberty is more than a power to vote. In practice, in the real world, it is the ground of all liberty. It is not only the fortress of the free spirit, but its home. When it is lost the people, even before they feel oppression, lose the sentiment of liberty. They do not feel life with the same zest ; their very arts become forced or languid, like the pleasures of the rootless.

Above all, as experience has shown, without political liberty freedom is not safe. Autarchies have sometimes given liberty to the mind, but most—nowadays all—use censorship and attempt by special education to form children to pattern.

A standard index for education, dealing with averages, would not show this. Statistics of boards of education give only a standard of comparison between schools and countries ; they cannot tell us how far each child has realized its power, how far it has made actual growth in mind and character. Statistics cannot measure character. Yet this is the vital distinction between the democratic and autarchic states, that the first stand upon the unique personality of each subject and the second despise or deny it.

103. It is a danger inherent in norms that they are taken for reality. They stand between reality and the man, so that he is committed, by abstract thought, to all kinds of absurdity. Clock time, for instance, a true norm, is often mistaken for a real thing. African travellers who discovered that the native calendars contained only 270 or 300 days cried, "Oh, the poor ignorant savages—no wonder they remain poor and wretched !" and tried to teach them the Christian calendar. Whereas the natives, of course, had a real calendar. They started their year with the first shower of rain and ended it with harvest. After that they amused themselves with hunting until the next real year began.

The illusion that clock time is real derives probably from the clock-face, where the hand is seen to move continuously across one mark after another. This leads to such metaphors as the passage of time. Real time does not pass. It simply adds to itself. It creates the present. Man grows old, but it is useless to measure the process by hours and minutes. His different organs age at different rates.

Another odd notion from the same source is that the present does not exist. The second hand, apparently, does not stop anywhere. From this arises the argument that man has, in fact, no present, that he has no permanent self. So man is abolished, in theory, by his own clock-work tool. But man's self, of course, has the same kind, though not the same degree, of permanency as the character of any element, iron or oxygen, maintained by a continuous activity of atoms in that character.

Eddington has pointed out that in the same way all scientific standards, which are measurements, tend to hide, even from scientists, the fact that they are not dealing directly with reality, but with measurements.

But it is precisely the artificial and ideal character of clock time which makes it independent of the irregularity and unpredictable vagaries of real things and enables it to be used, throughout the world, for the organization of transport and science. Its value to real liberty is incalculable, even in such by-ways as the Daylight Saving Act.

104. No standard, no norm can measure the personality. But where political liberty is real and secure and where there is freedom of the mind, such a standard of integration, even if it were possible, is not needed. No one

needs statistics to compare Athens with Sparta or nineteenth-century France with nineteenth-century Turkey. But even these comparisons are false, because they compare averages, and character is not subject to average. We might say that country X had a thousand great men to one from country Y, but that the second is a thousand times greater than all the first put together ; but no one could prove it. Which is greater, Plato or Pasteur, Goethe or Beethoven ? There is no sense in the question.

A standard of mensuration can apply to quantities but not qualities. It can grade the liberties of the people only by their economic power, their hours of work and leisure, their standards of education, their votes, and their freedom to know.

105. The character of reality itself, its final being, is not to be measured. Yet science, which is mensuration, gives us useful truth about it.

The insurance agent, when he agrees to pay you a thousand pounds on your death, does not foretell your future. You may be run over within half an hour. He does not predict the fate of any individual, and if he did he would be trusting to luck and not to science. He predicts only for a great number of people taken together, and he relies upon an average, which is a third thing, a norm. It is a measurement depending on facts which are beyond the control of any individual or any state at any one time. Without this norm insurance would be impossible, for no one could compare risks or predict anything of the future. What is certain in the average is merely probability in the individual. When we compare Athens with Sparta, nineteenth-century Turkey with France, and judge that under democracy every kind of greatness in invention, commerce, the arts must flourish we are not arguing that a certain man who in Sparta or Turkey came to nothing would in Athens or France have certainly achieved greatness, but only that all men in those countries have greater opportunities. Power, security, and freedom were given to them, but they did what they chose. Nobody can claim for Greece or France, "I made this glory" ; but Cleisthenes and Rousseau might say, "I gave to man the power of making his own glory."

106. Those who battled with the state in the name of liberty have been especially fearful for the liberty of genius. Men like Mill, of original mind and power, could never forget for an instant that during thousands of years authority has been the deadliest enemy of an original mind. They could not forget the fate of Socrates, of Christ, of Bruno, and Galileo,

of every original artist and poet. They looked upon all states, all churches, and all academies as the natural destroyers of genius.

It is, of course, true that states, churches, and academies have always feared and hated genius. Whether they are controlled by ambitious egotists who seek only power and security for themselves or by honest men sincerely believing that there is only one true faith, one scientific creed, one good art in the world, they detest the innovator. Men at the head of institutions are necessarily of mature age, with settled convictions and ideas. Such men, even if they should be geniuses, do not welcome new facts and arts which tend to supersede their own. They are unfitted to understand them. They honestly regard them as ridiculous or false or dangerous to society. But for every great poet, artist, or scientist murdered by authority millions have died of neglect.

Shelley was free by the old theorists ; so is the composer who starves in a slum and whose work will never be produced.

107. The liberty of genius is not a special lack of restraint to which genius is entitled. It is absurd to say, "Blake ought to have enjoyed special immunity from the law because he was a genius," but it is good sense to say, "Blake, because he was a genius, should have had every

help from the state to realize his extraordinary
powers, for the state's own good." Genius
is entitled to a special liberty, to special education, to special help and opportunity.* Many
states already give that education and help.
For three hundred years France has given
real liberty to artists. She has paid from the
taxes large sums that young painters might have
power to achieve themselves. She has therefore given to the world more great painters than
any other nation.

President Roosevelt through his W.P.A.,
Federal Arts, and Federal Theatre schemes has
given to thousands of writers, actors, artists,
and composers the power to work.† These
men accept state aid and undertake in return
a duty to society. They must produce, within
fixed times, work satisfactory to the committees
in charge of their districts. Such a scheme
would have shocked an old liberal. But which
has real liberty, an artist starving in the bread
line, without materials, without hope, or one
with a secure income, a brush in his hand and
a canvas or a wall in front of him ?

Which scientist has more freedom—he who
has the key of the street or he who is given a
laboratory for research ?

---

* So, of course, is everybody else, according to his powers.
† 150,000 artists, actors, composers, and playwrights were lately on
the rolls.

108. Authority may still be stupid and oppressive. The state or the university may criticize the scientific results ; the local committee of W.P.A. may not recognize a work of genius submitted for its approval. It is a matter of history that France, having by great expense given herself such artists as Monet, Renoir, and Cézanne, did not perceive that they were artists at all and took every means to discourage them. The French Salon, in fact, has been even more hostile to the original artist than the English Academy. But this is only a proof, if anyone needed proof, that artists and scientists make bad bureaucrats. The cure for bad administration is not anarchy but enlightenment. Bureaucrats are also men. They have the liberty of reason. They are not bound to folly, even though they may have practised it for five thousand years. It is said that the committees of the American arts scheme have shown themselves, on the whole, as wise as any of the rich amateurs who, at different times, have given artists liberty to paint what they chose. So that they have shown much more intelligence than any salon or academy known to the old world.

109. Liberty of genius is not a special case. All liberty is social and has the same relation with society and the state. The artist takes for

his material the whole product of all other artists and relies for appreciation upon an audience that could not exist except in a society providing liberty for artists. On the other hand, the state or the state organ, whether academy or department, which tries to dictate to artists what they shall paint or scientists what they shall find is wasting its money and making besides a great fool of itself. It is taking its place beside Galileo's judges, the Salon which refused Cézanne for thirty years, and the English Academy which drives out the artist of genius and accepts his imitators.

110. The nature of liberty itself makes absurd that other bogey of the Victorian anarch, uniformity. Mill imagined a world in which state action had crushed out all difference of opinion, of character ; in which everyone dressed, spoke, believed, and behaved exactly like all the rest. Even to-day there are writers and speakers who, blind or deaf to the real world which whirls about them in increasing tumult, calmly declare that society is in danger of regimentation. If Mill were brought from the eighteen-fifties to a modern bathing-beach or night club, to a modern university or to modern towns, he would not be anxious about the variety of life. But state organization has increased beyond Mill's greatest fears.

The true criticism of a modern public school, certainly of the greater schools, is not that they turn out a uniform product but that they cater for so many differences of taste and character among boys that they have no time for sound instruction in first principles. The secondary schools tend to a more uniform product, but that is because they take their scholars from a class with less liberty, both of mind and body. The remedy is more liberty for that class, more pay, more travel, better education, more books, more holidays, more ideas about a real world known by actual experience.

111. To organize the devolution of liberty to individuals that can use it is all that society can do for its own health and progress. If it wants discoveries, it must build laboratories and endow scientists ; if it wants great art, it must build art schools and theatres and opera-houses and see that artists and playwrights and actors, singers and composers have the same hope of employment and livelihood as clerks or soldiers. But equally, if it wants great discoveries and great works of art, it must not define what it wants.

True greatness, the honour of achieving in the world and for the world some permanent conquest of the truth, some lasting beauty, is within the reach of any state which organizes its economy to that end. But it must have faith in the spirit which breathes and works in liberty. So far as existing states do show faith, or so far as they are compelled by democratic power to respect liberty, they are rewarded in progress. So far as they repress liberty and use education to deceive, censorship to prevent original thought and art, they prepare for themselves contempt and ruin. For the wealth and glory of a state is simply the realized liberty of its people, and no man can realize himself except in his own character.

The real question of politics, underlying all other temporary questions, is not, How shall the world be ruled? but, How shall democracy be organized for its own security and for the best results? That is to say, how are we to achieve the greatest liberty of the greatest number?

CHAPTER VI

Democracy, Historical

112. The theory of democracy has usually been founded on natural right or the moral freedom. The conception is that of men born into a world without government or social obligation. In fact, democracy arose from power. Primitive men have never existed without social relations. The earliest society, prehuman in origin, was the patriarchal family. Such a family is the root both of autocracy and democracy. When it increased into the tribe under a patriarchal chief descended from the original patriarch, it was the origin of monarchy. Kings are still called fathers of their people. But sometimes family groups remained small, each under its own patriarch. This happened when a people made settled farms. In Africa it has been noticed also among professional hunters, who choose to live in small groups close to their game. Wherever small patriarchal families grew up side by side, scattered through woods or on fertile patches among the hills, there was a conflict of powers, of sovereigns.

In actual history, for instance in early Greek history, such families usually derived from a former tribal horde which had split up on settling to their homesteads. Thus there remained to them common traditional law, and the heads of families in their quarrels could appeal to such a law. Any of them who knew that law or could interpret it was likely to acquire special authority. But it was authority among masters, it was authority to interpret rather than to judge, and it did not encroach upon the patriarchal authority of family heads. Even in the Roman empire as late as A.D. 300 the master of the family had nominal power of life and death over his children. He had the essential power and function of a king—to judge and to punish even to death.

113. Thus in Greece and Rome the first democracies were not folk meetings but the committee of patriarchs, the assembly of kings, men whose real power was grounded in the family and in property.

The reason why democracy, from the rule of the village elders and patriarchs, came in cities to be the rule of the citizens is long and complex. Many influences worked in cities to break up the large household—to oblige sons on marriage to build far from the paternal home, to bring in new households of strangers. The same tendencies can be seen to-day in Africa, where every stage of the social development exists side by side : the tribe, the large patriarchal household, the village in which half a dozen such families live together, each giving an elder to the council which spends sometimes a whole day ascertaining traditional law or trying to fit some new event into its stiff forms ; and the town, where patriarchs survive as chief citizens, as a local nobility ; beside the huts of immigrant traders and workers, where the family group is man, wife, and children and the patriarch is a day-labourer.

114. When patriarchs have sunk to citizens and labourers, they easily lose their liberty. They have lost the real power of the family group, which was in property and in the men to defend it. But also, if they remember their dignity as house masters, if tradition give them real power in their own households, however small, above all, if they are a people naturally brave and energetic, men born to liberty and power, they will band together to secure themselves against the tyrant. They will breed men who look upon democracy as the right and glory of the race. Thus Solon and Cleisthenes in Greece, when the tyrants had threatened the liberties of the people, deliberately set themselves to devise constitutions which would defend

their liberties and enable men of real power to join together in the efficient direction of the state.

These were the first democratic constitutions in the world. They were founded on this idea, that power should be with the citizens of full age and capable of bearing arms to defend their liberties. It was not to be mob rule, but the actual government of responsible men.

These first constitutions were based on the vote, which has ever since been the ground of political liberty. There is no other means by which numbers can make the single acts of will necessary to any policy.

115. It is often said that one vote among millions cannot have the power to decide any issue, and that therefore the very idea of political liberty is false and democracy a fraud. This is to misunderstand the vote, which is a relation between the people and the state. All relations have two ends. At the voters' end the relation is one of responsibility. Each man, however little his separate power, knows that it is real power. Those who seek his vote are called candidates and behave like suppliants. They come to him for his vote, as in autarchies petitioners come to the actual rulers of the state and he grants it of his own will. However careless or stupid such a man may be, he has

the sense of mastership. In old democracies this feeling of power is so much the common air that it is not noticed. In such countries political liberty is a climate that no one cares for until it is threatened or lost. But the difference is felt like a change of the seasons, which penetrates the whole life and alters the very ground of it.

The whole thought of a people having this liberty is pregnant with the force of it, which is to make and to do. Their talk wherever it is heard has the ring of masters. They speak of governments as of an inferior race of slaves, abusing them with royal contempt or taking their part with the affectionate encouragement that a king gives to his willing fool. Democratic arrogance is a by-word in Europe—self-assertion, presumption, the indifference of mandarins to local opinion. A stupid Englishman or American behaves as if it was his birthright to know all that is worth knowing and to be the centre of every company. These are the typical faults of the stupid duke. They spring from a sense of power and the flattery of courtiers.

These courtiers in a democratic country are the actual rulers. They flatter perhaps, like other courtiers, with their tongues in their cheeks, but they are not playing a game. They know where the power is. Anyone who opens a paper in England, America, or France can read columns in which the flattery, implied or direct, lies like a glittering frost of sugar. Since woman had a vote new flatteries are aimed at her. A comparison between a newspaper to-day and the same sheet about twenty-five years ago will show how greatly woman's courtiers have increased since she came into power.

116. The flattery of the voter, at election time, is necessary to obtain from him a delegation of power. Governments having obtained that power are then supposed to ignore him. Rousseau said that England had liberty only during a general election. This is the typical mistake of an abstract thinker. Just as the possession of a vote profoundly affects the whole character and feeling of a man, not only in political relations but throughout his activities, so the existence of many millions of voters has a continuous effect upon a government. But what in one voter is a minute fraction of power is in groups and parties a sovereign capable of destroying governments. The government's relation to the voter is not that of the ministry to a single man, but of the state to millions of men and masters, each directing upon it their watchful and changeable wills. The relationship of king and courtier is not changed, as Rousseau imagined, when the courtiers go to

Parliament ; only its action is changed. A private member may grow careless of his promises, but a cabinet finds itself in the position of a single courtier serving several million kings.

It is the fashion to say that modern centralized government, and especially its bureaucracy, has taken so much power from the people that governments need not mind them. To judge by such recent events as the resignation of Sir Samuel Hoare,* this is not true. It is easy to think so, no doubt, so long as liberty is imagined as absence of restraint, or, what usually follows from that definition, as merely political ; but the fact is that the people's total power and the energy of their political thought has increased more quickly than the counter-power of the bureaucracy. Thus in England democracy is probably stronger internally than it was even fifteen years ago. It carries more weight of determination and more power to put that will into effect.

When it fails to move the government the reason is not in its weakness but its division. It was united upon housing, and therefore successive governments and municipal councils have pushed forward the clearance of slums. It was divided about war—between those who

* Upon the Hoare-Laval agreement to partition Abyssinia.

wished to fight for the League and those who wouldn't fight for any cause ; and so the policy of the government has been uncertain and confused. It is because democracy is powerful that its confusions and divisions are mirrored in the government policy. Palmerston would have acted in a different manner from Baldwin or Chamberlain because he was in actual fact more independent.

CHAPTER VII

Democracy, Organization, Political

117. Society does not run itself in any part of the world. Tribal organization is not an automatic machine ; it is a net of powers delegated by fixed laws to men and women, who thereupon undertake the task of government. This task must be undertaken wherever society exists. An English farm does not run itself, nor can it be run from a distance by schedule or fixed rules. There must be some man on the spot, to look at the weather and the state of the soil, to know what tasks should be done and what can be done.

The farmer, however small his farm, and every woman who organizes her household, the hours of her shopping, her mending, her children's meals and bed-times, are a part of the real government in any country. All do not govern, because all do not take responsibility or give pains to the duty. Every class carries its drifters ; born parasites who will not take the trouble to manage even their own affairs.

But nine households in ten throughout the country, from the poorest to the richest, have responsible governors, men and women who take some thought for the contriving of the good life, as they imagine it, within their own reach of power.

118. Real social organization is universal, but it is personal government. The farmer knows his men, his horses, his cows, what they can do and what is wrong or right with them. The mother of a family changes her arrangements every day to meet the crises of family organization—sickness, tempers, treats, and parties. It is an odd thing that the mothers of families and the mistresses of households, who have daily experience of the real difficulties of government, of the management of human beings, should be commonly the most dogmatic and abstract critics of state government. It might be thought that their minds are dogmatic because their government is personal and despotic ; but in practice it will be noticed that those women who are least inclined to despotism are most contemptuous of ministers and party leaders. The reason is probably that they reason unconsciously like anarchists, who, finding love and good will in their own hearts and happiness in their own families, look upon all the evils of life as the invention of the state.

119. Social organization is the positive nexus of society. It is diffused government, the natural and necessary political democracy which is the ground of all government. But even in early times the personal organization of the household was supplemented by the central organization of justice, and after justice security. The conflicts of freedom within society produced the need of law, or fixed rules independent of personal influence. These laws required a central executive, judges, and police.

120. Such judges were the first bureaucrats, and their function was to stand outside personal real government. They administered law not according to the person but the tradition. The earliest judges were, in fact, the most strict in their disregard of personal factors, of equity, and in their respect for the letter of the law. The primitive lawgiver, priest or priest-king, sitting among his people, knew the people individually, and he had his own sympathies ; but he gave out the law as an inflexible and impersonal doom. The modern bureaucrat sitting in his office with a deputation lays down the rule according not to the hard cases before him, but to the statistics of his department.

For this reason man, understanding from his own experience that justice and efficiency, dealing with real people, both require personal knowledge and reject *a priori* rules, hates the bureaucrat, who seems to him rather a tyrannical robot than a free man.

121. Modern government under all systems has a bureaucratic executive, and many speak and think as if this form of organization were something new and extraordinary in the world, an invention of despots. But it is as old as central government itself and a natural product of organization, which is essential to all societies, including the democratic.

122. It is useless to hinder or attack the growth of bureaucracy in modern states. It is not the cause but the consequence of the increasing complexity of organization necessary to modern society. Creative liberty by its natural growth, its sudden development of new demands, new problems, compels organization. Moreover, this pressure of liberty upon the framework of the state must increase. Scientific research has only begun to give returns. It is still poorly endowed. There will, in the future, be more not less invention, cheaper means of production. The state that fails to contrive new organs to distribute the new wealth will be smashed.

Moreover, as Marx saw, the forces which drive economic society forward are beyond the control of any individual or state. They can only be directed, guided, and the direction requires not only imagination in rulers, but expert knowledge in their technical advisers.

Organization must and will increase as the powers of the people, improved by education, gather force. All states stand between organization and revolution. In any case bureaucracy will grow. In democracy it is the chief internal danger, the chief potential enemy of the people's liberty.

123. The reason is that bureaucracy, by nature, deals not with real people but with statistics and rules. Rules do not change and statistics deal with averages. But people change and none of them conforms to an average. A bureaucracy tends to a kind of oppression which, if it is not so dangerous in immediate effects as that of a single tyrant or a party, may be more destructive in the long run. It may kill the inventive genius of a people.

Liberty cannot be destroyed and it always creates. But much of that creation, for instance among insects, is repetitive. The people make new things, but in the exact image of the old. Of course, the most primitive do sometimes invent, or civilization, even as we know it, would never have appeared ; but the progress was slow.

Bureaucracy fills the place of an absolute

tribal law, governing by tradition. Its effects can be seen in China, where one of the earliest civilized races in the world, governed by an academic bureaucracy, gradually fell into stagnation.

124. These effects are much more definite and direct than many people imagine. Anyone who has had to do with a government office knows the difficulty of changing its age-old ideas and routine. Anyone who has experience of government service—for instance, a colonial service—where all the departments are bureaucratic and the whole state machine may be described as socialistic or bureaucratic, has the most vivid impression of this defect.

Such a service has great virtues. It is disinterested, it is not corrupted by the meaner ambitions, it seeks the welfare of the community, because that is its job, for which it is paid and rewarded. But it has equally no inducement, from ambition or pay, to experiment, to take the risk and trouble of innovation.

Bureaucracy, therefore, though essential to government, is itself unfitted to rule. It cannot fulfil the essential duty of a ruler, to support and encourage liberty of invention. Its function is to execute the will of actual rulers.

125. The actual rulers of an autarchy are easy to distinguish. In theory, at least, one rules

Germany. But in a democracy it is not so easy to find the ruler. The Cabinet, in England, is subject to Parliament and Parliament to the electors. The power of the electors is real not only at the end of election, but continuously.

Any experienced politician will tell you how surprisingly the temper of the House can change between Friday and Monday. A case well received on the first day may be shouted down on the second. The reason is that during their usual week-end visits to their constituencies M.Ps. have found that the weight of popular opinion is against it. This occurs where the mass feeling of the electors has an obvious and definite object. But the continuous pressure, which cannot be seen so closely in action, is even more strongly effective. Any large body of popular feeling has a continuous effect on policy in two ways : it checks any legislative action which might offend it, because party managers warn ministers of its existence ; it encourages, for the same reason, any action pleasing to it. A minister who is casting about for popularity or a member who is looking for votes knows very well where to find them.

126. But such unorganized bodies of opinion in order to be effective must be both

large and single-minded. A very large body of opinion in England wants peace, and their influence is strong. Large numbers want improved education for children, but they have no agreement about policy. The government, therefore, in questions of education does not consider this vague, unorganized desire ; it is to be influenced only by the pressure of organized bodies expressing their will in plain terms. Such a body is the National Union of Teachers ; another is the British Medical Association.

Both these bodies stand between the single teacher or doctor, weak in isolation, and the state. Such organized groups are the most important means by which modern democracy exerts its will upon the state.

127. A trade union, a peace league, touring club, medical association are essential organs of democratic and representative government. They are more truly representative of the citizen than the elected member. The reason is this. A man with a single vote in a constituency of thirty thousand has the choice of two or perhaps three members, each with a programme. The programmes differ, no doubt, in their main principles, but they are extremely vague in detail. A voter is lucky who finds any one of them completely in agreement with his own

views ; and even then, he is only asked to decide general principles.

But if the same man belongs, let us say, to a trade union, or trade association, a cyclists' or motorists' league, a benefit society, the Anglers' Association and the Footpath Society, he exerts through each a direct power upon government which exactly represents his will in each department of action.

For instance, as a miner he wants not only certain improvements in pay and hours, which belong to the general policy of his party, but he is interested in special safety regulations ; in the operation of a steel cartel, as affecting prices of coal ; in a thousand details of policy important only to miners. His trade union expresses his will in these details. But as a nonconformist he is interested in education. His party has a general programme for education, but he wants special consideration for his own schools. His church organization, through its paid secretaries and central officials, will express his will in these details. As a fisherman injured by the pollution of rivers he acts through the Anglers' Association with all the power belonging to millions of fishermen.

In each case his act of will, unlike a political vote, is simple and fully expressive. It is also in continuous operation, because it is carried out by paid officials of the union, association, or club, whose only duty it is to affirm that will and to strive by every means to make it effective.

128. Thus this man, apart from his political vote, is represented in actual politics by a group of active powers which taken together are exactly correspondent to his individual character. They are truly representative of that man and only of that man. For his neighbours in the same street, men doing the same work and belonging to the same political party, no two have the same group representation. One is a Roman Catholic, his hobbies are music and football ; another belongs to the Lord's Day Observance Society and the Welsh nationalist party ; and another is local secretary for the League of Nations Union and Repertory Theatres Guild. If each of these men could be pictured in his actual political character not merely as a voter but in the personal form which exerts his full power in society, one would see a leviathan much more positive in power and true in representation than Hobbes's abstract portrait of the absolute state. For each organ of each leviathan is an actual composite thing, a league, union, club, whose working is as clearly defined and continuous as any real organ of the body, and the leviathan itself, operating with the force of thousands or even millions of men, represents

one man, possibly a very modest and obscure citizen, in his own character. Moreover, it is always at work. The man himself may give little thought to his own interests, but the giant which he has called up to work for him never thinks of anything else and toils night and day in his service.

129. The group organ is the chief means by which the individual in a democratic state can express his personal will and secure his personal liberty against bureaucracy. For he uses against state bureaucracy the very power of bureaucracy itself, its persistence, its rigid devotion to a task laid down for it. His bureaucrats, his office secretariat, give him the same devoted service for the same reason, because it is their job. If his bureaucrats show the typical vices of their kind, in narrow-mindedness and stagnation, he can and does act towards them as actual ruler. He can change them or harry them, for the man who pays the wages commands the policy. In practice this is usually done by forming new and more active societies to prod or supersede the old ones. Trade unions are continually thwarted and prodded by such new organizations.

If a man cannot find in existing organs the right combination to represent his whole will, he can set about making new ones. This is done every day. Every new hobby, new trade, new game, political theory, religious sect, health cure produces its association, its representative organ.

130. The group organs exert their pressure directly on society and on government by propaganda in the press and letters or deputations to ministers and members of Parliament. These in turn command the state bureaucrat.

This relation between the ministers and the groups has become a very important part of the organization of actual government. It is often quite as valuable to ministers as to the representative groups. The success of a minister is often in direct proportion to his personal relations with those who can make him learn directly how large bodies of men feel and think on any question.

The vote is the basis of all political democracy, but the group is its most powerful weapon of fulfilment. It is therefore the first thing destroyed by an autarchy, which either abolishes all unions and groups or adapts them to its own purpose.

To abolish the power of free associations is to destroy the essence of the modern democratic organization. To turn such associations into corporations and call the product a co-operative state is to change the living and changing body of group organs into a steel frame within which each member is representative merely of formal character, and the whole is a structure of averages, the purest bureaucratic abstraction.

Liberty of association is the central fortress of political democracy, and it should be jealously defended. But if it be taken from men legally, they will form their clubs and leagues in secret.

CHAPTER VIII

Democracy, Organization, Economic

131. Economic organization of any society cannot be treated in abstraction. It is part of the general organization of liberty, which in a democracy includes political liberty. The difference between autarchies and democracies does not appear in an economic plan. The factory as a factory, transport as transport, has everywhere the same organization. The worker compared by rates of pay and leisure as an economic unit is the same quantity in Russia, Italy, or France. But the real worker, the real man, has in France political liberty. Therefore his real position is different and his real economic position is different, because he has the power to strike and also the appeal from his employer to the state.

Marx's analysis of society, as he himself points out, was abstract. But that is why it has failed to give any clue to the real events of history or guidance to rulers. In leaving out of account the political and social factors, the ideal and religious movements, in isolating the economic process, it missed the truth and became useless or dangerous even to the communist revolution. Marxism has nearly wrecked the workers' cause, which is in the nature of things democratic. It is not a dictatorship of the people, but rulership in people, a real liberty and power, which, being thwarted in the individual, takes unexpected revenge.

132. But Marx was right when he argued that the economic process was not to be controlled by laws or fitted into any preconceived idea of what society ought to be. This does not mean that a mysterious power superior to man has charged itself with the direction of society, but simply that man's possession of creative liberty makes that direction always new and unpredictable.

It is this fact which during the whole economic history of the world has finally changed or broken all economic systems. If the people have political power they use it to modify a system, as in the western democracies ; if they have not, and do not make a violent revolution to get it, they act upon it indirectly and often unconsciously. Production falls and there is a high level of bad work, or the workers leave one employment for another and the first has to be re-organized.

117

In Russia, unpopular factories lost workers so quickly that a law was made forbidding them to change their employment. Then production fell and the percentage of bad work tended to rise. To correct this, piece-rates were introduced, high pay was offered for the best workers, and competition was encouraged between different men and factories. These changes were made because they were to the advantage of the state and of society. A greater production made possible a higher standard of comfort and more liberty for everybody, including the authorities.*

133. Those who consider the economic system by itself make the same mistake as those who deal with politics or religion in isolation. The interaction between political and economic ideas and the facts beneath them is continuous in society, because it is continuous in men who form society. A man's economic interests are only a part and sometimes a small part of his complete interests.

134. A mass education and a rigid social plan of caste and class is possible only among primitive and illiterate peoples with little more than natural liberty, so that what is called a total economic plan can only be applied to the

* *The Good Society*, Lippman, p. 197 : "In a poor country the scarcity of capital, of special ability will make wages of capital and ability higher than in a country where they are more abundant."

lowest class of labour in a society still primitive. Even there it breaks down as soon as production requires or develops a class of skilled workers, that is to say, men whose individual quality demands special consideration. As a state which chooses to ignore creative intelligence in a people wastes it and suffers stagnation or ruin, so it will suffer if it attempts to use skilled labour or direction like the unskilled. The force of this platitude, known to a thousand years of employers and states, has been obscured by the idea that modern mass-production does away with skill and turns the worker into a helpless slave of the machine.

It is true that in those trades where the conveyor-belt can be used to hurry production workers often suffer the fact and sense of being driven. Their only remedy is political—to protest through their union or to strike.

Modern methods of production are not by themselves enemies of the worker. They can help or hinder according to their use. They can make work easier and more productive, therefore worth a better wage ; or they can make shorter hours possible without loss of production. They are part of a general organization of society which enables it to produce more wealth in a given time. The sharing of the wealth and leisure produced is controlled by the total organization—not merely the economic, but the political in the fullest sense.

135. But mass-production even in those factories where the conveyor-belt controls the chief part of the output requires also engineers, testers, foremen, managers, often research workers, who cannot be driven by the same methods. Yet the total efficiency of the production depends upon them.

In countries where the workers have liberty to change their employment a factory cannot afford to lose its trained men even from the belt ; in countries where they have not that liberty, it will suffer by their private hatred. There will be inefficiency and sabotage of that gradual, almost unconscious type that cannot be detected except over a period by a general deterioration of plant and waste of material. But the greater damage is again to the whole society. It cannot be separated and labelled economic. Where workers are treated like slaves, in so far as they are deprived of liberty, they will be open or secret enemies of the state. An autarchy which compels them to be secret will simply drive their hatred underground, where like a heath fire it will burn for years, undermining the whole earth with fire and ash.

The hatred of the workers does not seem

dangerous to autarchies. They govern in their factories, as in the state, by spies and terror ; it is a police government, and it breaks in the same way. At the first sign of weakness there is a revolution.

136. Organization, and especially factory organization, in all modern states, whether autarchic or democratic, has put power in the hands of workers. When that power has itself been organized, it can protect their liberties ; where it is not organized, it still consciously or unconsciously puts pressure on the state and modifies its plans. This pressure increases rapidly with any improvements in the workers' skill. It increased steadily in Russia from the time of the first re-organization of industry, when numbers of new peasants were brought into industry, till now when great modern factories employ thousands of skilled men. It is still increasing. Although probably the actual political power of the Russian worker is still small, his real liberty steadily advances. He has to be considered by his employer because his co-operation is needed and because experience shows that its value to the state is proportionate to its willingness.

137. Capitalism usually stands for owner-ship of the means of production. This is not an economist's definition, but a politician's.

Means of production include the total machine equipment of a state, its working capital, land, transport, minerals, and technical ability. But technical ability is in men, so that the state which absorbs all capital power must also control all its subjects. It must assume not only absolute economic but political direction. It becomes the dictator state. This leads, therefore, to the ordinary paradoxes and difficulties of absolutism.

In practice we have seen that Russia has begun to emancipate technical directors. It pays them higher wages and allows them special liberties. In course of time, whether communism survives or not, it is safe to say that they will be in a similar position to professional men in a democratic state.

But they will be wage-earners like professional men elsewhere, doctors, engineers, and directors, and if they own capital, it will be invested capital. That is to say, it will be a share in the total product of liberty, and not ownership of any means of production except their own skill, which cannot be nationalized.*

138. In practice and in all states technical directors and skilled workers are given the use of capital equipment, to make the best of it.

* I am ignoring the ordinary shareholders' control of company policy, which is almost negligible. Investment in government stock is already possible in Russia.

The better the equipment and the more liberty, including technical and commercial power, given to the directors, the better results are likely to be. Thus even under the communist state capital power is delegated in use. The state is in the position of a landlord who owns the land and manages its general interests like drainage and roads, but lets out the farms to individual experts according to the nature of the land and their own skill—meadows to dairy farmers, downs to the sheep men.

Each of these men has control or use of capital, sometimes his own, sometimes borrowed from a bank or the estate.

This is also the position in a totalitarian state. It must be so because of the nature of liberty in men. Of course, there may be more or less interference in the technical direction of any industry or factory from a minister, but that means only that a new director is wanted or a new minister. Either the director is not fit for his job or the minister is hindering him.

139. A director has control of capital for the use of his industry. He buys stock, machinery ; or builds new departments. The difference between a democratic state and a communist state is only in this, that in the former he owns the capital or borrows it from the public ; in the latter, he takes it from the

state. Abstractly, this difference is trifling ; in practice it is real and profound.

The relation of the state to the user of capital is an aspect of the relation between state and man. Thus it raises the same question : Which is master ? And produces the same theories : the autarchic and the anarchic. The autarchs in this case are the state capitalists, who say, "Society has produced all capital ; therefore it must have total power over capital." The anarchs are the private capitalists, who say, "Men make wealth ; therefore men shall dispose of all wealth."

Like the old theorists of the state, both parties ignore the real nature of the historical process, which does not obey any of their rules, and the real nature of liberty, which answers their problem by imposing itself on both. A centralized plan breaks down because it ignores the creative liberty of men ; the anarchic plan, such as we saw in Europe during much of the nineteenth century, breaks down because it ignores the necessity of state action to organize and secure liberty.

A private capitalist even under *laisser-faire* economics depended on acts of Parliament to give him railways over the land of private owners ; he owed all his means of transport directly to the state. He owed, also, most of his

124

processes to the invention of other people—
that is, to society ; and he found his workers and
his markets in society. Society, on the other
hand, owed its prosperity to his organizing ability.

140. The conflict, private capitalists against
state capitalists, could be solved by a norm :
"the greatest prosperity of the greatest number."
But this is abstract, because it treats men and the
states solely as economic factors. The real
norm is therefore the greatest liberty of the
greatest number, in which the economic index
represents the economic factors for wages,
hours, and leisure.*

141. State ownership of any means of
production is therefore part of the total problem
of the government. It cannot be treated in
isolation. For instance, it has been proposed
to nationalize the land. But the arguments
actually used on both sides are largely un-
economic. A strong argument comes from
those who want to preserve natural beauty for
the benefit of the whole people ; town-planners
want nationalization to make their work easy ;
and parents, teachers, and doctors support it
because in a planned countryside all children
would be taught among gardens and fields.

---

* This standard is actually used, by all those who urge special
limited technical education, to produce mechanics, doctors, engineers,
etc. Such education, to the Tsar Alexander II's great surprise,
produced abstract nihilists ; and produces now technocrats, sterilizers,
credit schemes, etc.

Arguments on the other side come from those who fear that the small man, whether farmer or householder, would suffer a loss of independence. They point out how already, in council estates, tenants are refused liberties which belong to private owners. They are supervised and inspected.

Meanwhile, during the battle of ideas, economic, sentimental, philosophic, and ethical, a new situation is arising in which the land is held partly for public use and partly remains in private control. The Mineral Rights Act, town planning acts, compulsory purchase acts, all strike a balance between public and private ownership. The new suggestion for national parks, by which large parts of the country could be reserved for the enjoyment of the whole people without loss of economic use to private owners, is a good example of the compromise arising directly not from any *a priori* theory but from the real nature of things—which is neither economic nor political. It follows that such a compromise is neither expensive nor dangerous.*

142. Thus there is reason to suppose that the land will finally be controlled by a complex and flexible system of ownership in which, as in every function of society, both natural liberty

* In the same way, the devolution of employment by the subsidy of trading estates and by private persuasion of employers arose directly from the problem and was the simplest answer to it.

and public need will take their part. The immense advantage of public control to town planning, road planning, to agricultural boards, afforestation, to the preservation of natural beauty and the setting aside of national parks, will be secured without the danger and oppression of direct bureaucratic control.

In the same way, all questions of state ownership—for instance, in the great industries—ought to be solved by references to the standard of a general liberty, and not to any *a priori* theory ; and they will be solved, sooner or later, by a course of events in which real men and real facts will be effective. That is to say, a bad or premature solution, a theoretical experiment, will produce evils which will oblige a correction ; or, by causing a general breakdown of efficiency, the ruin of the theorists who proposed it, the destruction of their party, and after more or less social confusion, an economic and political re-organization.*

143. Those who say production for profit must disappear are thinking abstractly or practising wish-fulfilment. Because they hate what they call the profit system, with its lies and noisy competition, they try to think that it must die. Profits are now the reward of

* These consequences are of course more severe in an autarchy, because its state machine is more rigid and more cut off, by the absence of free group organs, from the reality of people's needs and feelings.

127

successful competition. They are a premium paid by society for inventive and technical skill. If competition for profit be abolished, some other incentive plan has to be put in its place. In practice, the only other incentives are a direct reward or coercion. The former, a premium paid by the state, has neither the flexibility nor consistence of the profit system, which is always at work. The latter, coercion, is the ordinary method of autarchy, and it produces the same evils in industry as in the state.

144. Competition in itself is the result of liberty. For each man as creator makes his own world. No two men agree in all their powers, tastes, and opinions.

Competition and co-operation are both instinctive to men, they are both rooted in the nature of his liberty and freedom, and they are both essential means of his realization and his progress. Competition is the field of individual liberty ; co-operation is the field of social liberty.

In the real world they are not to be distinguished. All creative effort is at once competitive in some aspect and co-operative in another. The inventor is in competition with other inventors ; but in this work he uses an education, skill, and a total opportunity provided by society—that is, not only by all preceding inventors but by total history.

128

145. Competition without co-operation is anarchy ; co-operation without competition is impossible. The natural conflict produced by the natural action of liberty cannot be prevented ; it can only be shifted from one department to another—for instance, from economics to science or politics. The concentration of the whole energy of a people into the conflict for political power is a natural result of preventing economic competition.

146. Competition tends to a total economic efficiency, but uncontrolled it is a danger to individual liberty. The man who is ruined in the economic conflict is not an economic unit but a real man. That is why society is justified in protecting him from ruin ; unemployment insurance is not a dole. It is the acknowledgement of society that the man is more than a unit, that the economic system is only part of the organization of real society.

To abolish competition itself would not only fail to remove its dangers from the real life of a society, which is political as well as economic, but produce new dangers and new problems of organization.

The same problem exists in the examination system. It arises in the same way from the difference in individual power. It produces the same difficulty for society : to secure the advantages of different ability without injustice. If it were abolished, some other method would be needed to produce the same result ; therefore it would also be competitive and risk injustice.

147. Competition arises from the nature of society, but its social use is efficiency. Its counterpart is the co-operation which, by destroying competition in any one sphere of action, produces stagnation.

Thus combines and trusts may defeat both the purpose of competition and the interests of democracy by forming monopolies. They operate then as autarchies and produce the same evils. The only remedy in a democracy is political action. This has been used both in Britain and in the U.S.A. to examine monopolizing combines and to break them up.

The conflict is the same as that between man and state and governed by the same rules. In Britain combination has been refused to the banks, but actually enforced on the railways and collieries. In each case public interest was the criterion.

148. There is one department of economy in which companies, though still in competition, are driving out the small owner to the loss of the general good : the multiple shop, which is underselling the local shop.

The value of a local trade is more than

economic ; it is real. A centralized trade is injurious to the whole society in the same manner that centralized government is bad for democracy. It withholds experience in responsibility and contrivance.

The argument for the multiple shop is that it gives better service and cheaper goods : that restriction upon large-scale distribution would be not only damaging to the general wealth but difficult to carry out.

The same argument has been used to justify ranch-farming against the small-holder. The answer to it in Ireland and Denmark has been co-operation among the small producers.

Co-operation among small tradesmen for central buying, central departments of organization and research would give them the same efficiency as the multiple shop and enable them to compete with it.

This would not mean the control of separate shops and it would not prevent competition between different shops in the same town. It would mean only that the co-operators in each trade would own their own factories or buy their goods on a scale equally large with the great firms. They would take shares in the central organization exactly as small farmers own shares in a creamery or machinery society. Shares could be owned by actual traders in proportion to their capital, and dividends would be at a fixed rate.

Two drapers in the same town would not necessarily sell the same goods. They would select from the wholesale supply according to their personal forecasts of trade. It might be found good also that they should not be obliged to spend more than a fixed minimum at their co-operative wholesale store, so that they could, if they chose, buy outside it.

A central wholesale co-operative store would need a guarantee from the members of a minimum proportion of orders. The advantage of a co-operative system, including producers or middlemen and owners, is to give to the greatest number possible the full economic responsibility which belongs to management, and to obtain for society the efficiency which arises not only from individual capacity but the enterprise of hope.

149. The object of co-operative production among Danish and Irish farmers is to secure the advantages of large capital for the small owner. It makes small ownership efficient in the modern state, and strikes therefore a balance between the creative liberty of the men and the productive power of the state. But it came about not in answer to economic demand, which was satisfied by the large estate, but to democratic pressure.

132

The people desired ownership and the co-operative system was devised—in Denmark to make ownership possible for small-holders ; in Ireland to remove its evils.

Large estate farms, like combines in industry, might be more efficient economically, but they do not satisfy the desire to own. This desire issues in accumulation. It is the source of capital power. Rousseau and most of the anarchists have traced the origin of the state from the first origin of property, and since they hate the state and see in it the source of all the evils in society, they look upon property itself as an evil.

Although, as we saw, property is not the same thing as capital, when capital stands for the means of production, those who attack capitalism, as such, usually attack all property. The idealist, whether following Hegel or Bakunin or Tolstoy, has always imagined for his ideal community one in which all goods are held in common. Kropotkin draws many pictures of communal ownership. He sees in communism a natural and happy solution of conflict and envy.

150. Thus state socialists and anarchists, aiming at the fullest satisfaction of man's desires, deny one of the strongest.

The reasons are complex and arise partly from

historical accident, partly from subconscious motives. In history, property-owners have been the enemies of progress and property itself has seemed to corrupt men. The great evangelists of reform, like saints of religion, have been men naturally contemptuous of owning as well as of owners.

151. Marx himself found private possessions a nuisance, the need of them a hindrance to work. His followers have devised a state free of such obstacles to work, thought, and, as they felt it, enjoyment.

Whenever Marxian doctrine is put into practice, there is at once violent conflict between the government, aiming at pure communism, and the people, seeking realization in ownership. This conflict in a real society has obliged the Russian government to modify its abstract theory of an ideal society. Lately it has restored a form of peasant proprietorship even to collective farmers. This limited ownership has already increased production.

152. In Britain, the trade unionist, not following any theory but aiming at security for the worker and defence of his home, has urged the distribution of employment. He knows that derelict towns mean broken homes and ruined lives. Factories are now actually built and building to meet this new demand. Em-

ployers are encouraged to take their works to the unemployed ; and not to wait for the unemployed to come to them. Thus a man's attachment to his home is acknowledged to have more force than purely economic laws.

153. This expedient of practical democrats, barely noticed by theoretical writers or politicians, is in fact of decisive importance. It means a new economic structure of society. The proletariat, as a fluid labour mass without roots, is about to disappear.

154. As usual when a new stage of the historical process shows itself, it is discovered to be the product of converging forces which seemed to have little interconnection. Unemployment pay was meant simply to relieve suffering, the trading estates to save derelict towns and their social equipment. They combine to fix workers and employment. But all the motives at work derive from human demands and man's persistence in seeking to satisfy them.

155. These demands are always for liberty, security, and the means of realization. But ownership is the means by which not only men but animals and birds realize their strongest instincts—of love, creation, dignity, and liberty.

156. Those who acknowledge the force and drive of this instinct are wont to say, "Pugnacity

is natural to man and beast, but that is no reason to foster it. If pugnacity must be restrained, why not the instinct to possess ?"

157. The objections urged against ownership are chiefly these : it is against the public good ; it is economically unsound ; it promotes private selfishness.

The first objection is aimed at capitalism. This has been dealt with already (see para. 137).

The economic objection is well founded. A nation of small owners shows great resistance to centralized control. This may be harmful to the society. A real conflict emerges which can only be solved by the norm of liberty. But liberty does not demand the abolition of ownership, only that it should be controlled or modified in the interest of general liberty.

158. The third objection, that ownership promotes conservatism, is true. It is urged, therefore, by all those who believe that the only remedy for social injustice is what they call the continuous revolution : a continuous struggle of the proletariat against the owners. They urge the breaking of agreements, sudden strikes, and violence in order to disorganize society and force it to make a new order.

But, as Bertrand Russell points out, continuous disorder in any society does not necessarily bring about the emancipation of the workers. It is more likely to produce a government resolved to preserve order at all costs, and the workers will pay most of the cost.

159. In fact, the idea of continuous revolution arises from an abstract notion of society, which does not consist of workers and directors, but of real people, each with his own trade, his own knowledge, experience, and tastes. All these real people are suffering or provoking change. They grow old, they obtain promotion, they better or worsen themselves. This is the true continuous revolution which takes place, quickly or slowly, in all societies. If it is too slow for the needs and ambitions of living people, they break the frame of that society. If it is too quick, the frame may break down of itself. But when the frame is broken, by any means, the continuous revolution comes to an end. A new society must be organized, usually by violent means. In this society the same men, for the most part, will fill the same kind of parts. Miners will be needed in mines, clerks in offices, directors, doctors, research workers all in their former places. But they will usually find themselves worse off than before. For history shows that society takes more force to drive after the damage of a breakdown than before. Any given social framework, a factory, an office, a family, a state, once thrown out of gear, com-

monly requires despotic control to set it once
more in working order.

Tyrannies are ephemeral. The workers destroyed in a social collapse, brought about by any
means, are succeeded by a new generation which,
in the frame of the new order, begins to exert
the old pressure. The continuous revolution
begins again, in the same direction, towards
economic and political power. But meanwhile
a generation has been thrown away.

160. The class war as a war-cry of the
continuous revolution is equally founded in
abstraction. It neither exists in any real society
nor can it be made to exist. The real conflict
is between groups which form a cross-section of
classes. For instance, there has always been
conflict between producers and consumers ;
between the country workers who want good
prices for their crops and town workers who
need cheap food ; miners producing coal or ore
and steel workers using it. Moreover, the
finished product of one trade is the raw material
of another. This conflict exists in every society,
whether democratic or communist. Practical
trade unionists know how much time they spend
in dealing with such problems. The notion of
class war is useless to them. It has no applica-
tion to the question, "What is a fair apportion-
ment of wages between this trade and that ?"

Equality of wage is no solution for unequal work and responsibility. In Russia it led to the desertion of unpleasant or dangerous trades and a shortage of foremen. The tendency now in all nations, whatever their political label, seems to be towards a complex standard : varying rates built upon an invariable equal minimum. In the index of economic liberty, this minimum should have more importance than the average rate.

161. The notion of a class war has been ruinous to the Marxists. It inspired their refusal in Italy, Germany, and Spain to co-operate with the democratic parties. Thus they ruined both these parties and themselves.

For the class war, when preached as a theory, does divide society, not into classes but into two groups : those who can profit by violence and disorganization and those who must suffer for it.

But in an organized state with its real democracy, the first class is very small. It includes only the criminal classes and possibly some of the unemployed, in so far as they see no hope of employment. To all the rest, violence is not only a nuisance but a danger. They fear for their jobs and their homes. This was the reality against which the Marxist group broke in Italy, Germany, and even Spain, primitive as it was : that in a class war the party imagined as the proletariat, but what is actually the party of violence, is in a great minority. It will always be defeated.

162. The class war doctrine is not directly dangerous to any existing democracy, but indirectly it is dangerous because it provokes a reaction of much greater power and violence than it could ever command. This reaction easily falls under the leadership of the enemies of democracy itself.

163. Thus the desire for power, even for possession, which is necessarily limited, does not involve a final conflict. The final ideal object, of the greatest possible power shared among all, can be obtained only by co-operation and adjustment. Trade unions make peace more often than war, and the total result of their work, over a hundred years, has been appeasement. This has been achieved in two ways ; by continuous adjustment of disputes and by an actual devolution of wealth. This distribution, though it leaves a huge inequality of power, has by itself enormously increased the general security and contentment.

164. The reason why the small security provided by unemployment insurance, rent restriction acts, and the increased standard of ownership has had such striking effects, even

in the last thirty years, is precisely that men do not think or live in terms of conflict, but of realization. They are even too easily satisfied with what they have. Small-holders work twelve or fourteen hours a day for a return far less than the wages of a labourer. Anyone who knows an owning peasantry anywhere in the world knows their dignity and patience, their lack of envy and their delight in hospitality. Anyone who visits the artisan and factory worker in their own homes finds the same good will and good humour, a generosity of mind often embarrassing to richer men. The crude violence of the battle is not that of individuals, but of groups and their advocates, whose business and duty it is to fight for justice.

For millions, poverty is so narrow that it is felt like a cell ; it is a continuous pressure upon the mind.* It injures, but it does not kill the mind or the powers of imagination. They may find their only opening in football pools or dog-racing, but they are there to support some dignity, some creative action necessary to the living soul. Even the balance of groups is not entirely a balance of the limited powers. Nations like the U.S.A., a millionaire in international society, and like Denmark, which is the peasant, have also renounced the idea of conflict.

* See *Men Without Work*. Cambridge University Press, 1938.

Groups are no more blind and stupid than individuals. They can also realize themselves rather in possession than conquest. Thus, given possession and some security, ownership tends as much to appeasement as conflict.

In theory it also tends to conservatism. Devolution of ownership and employment together, such as we see beginning in England and perhaps also in Russia, might in theory produce highly rigid and conservative societies. In practice, once a high standard of living and leisure is obtained, in a modern state with easy and quick transport, the evils of complacence and stagnation are not likely. In such a state ownership would be the firm ground of democracy and independence.

This is why it is attacked by one party, the state-socialist, and supported by another, the democratic and the trade unionist. The attitude of the man depends on his idea or theory of what society should be and what a state is for.

CHAPTER IX

Democracy, Dangers Peculiar to

165. Democracy is natural government because liberty is natural power. It will therefore be the government to which all states tend as they develop. But this does not mean that it is a formula for peace and security or that any specific democratic state is safe from collapse or destruction.

Democracy has greater strength than any autarchy. It can stand much greater tension and disorder. It has astonishing power of recovery after defeats, which always destroy an autarchy. But it owes this power to a division of real government.

This division is itself the consequence of liberty and the means of progress. As scientific division of power, in the form of laboratories, scholarships, endowments, makes for scientific progress, so the division of political power in the form of wealthy parties, trusts, unions, and associations is the means of political experiment and progress.

But division of power carries with it special dangers peculiar to democracy.

166. Real division of power exists in all states. In autarchies it is hidden, in democracies open. Ambitious men, the only men who undertake the drudgery of government anywhere, are necessarily opposed in interest. They seek friends, openly or secretly, and form cliques to advance their private power.

The important difference between autarchy and democracy is that the conflict for power, in the first, involves the whole safety of the state and the lives of the battlers. Party heads in England and America do not need to murder each other, because their lives are not risked in the issue. Roosevelt did not send his opponents to the concentration camp. Daladier has not caused Blum to be shot. But in Russia if Stalin had not destroyed the plotters against him, they would have destroyed him and his party. Hitler was obliged to destroy Roehm.

167. The essential weakness of democracy does not arise, as in autarchies, from the conflict of real power, but from the division of actual power. Conflict between different government parties may produce a deadlock, as in France.

Such a deadlock does not destroy or disorganize a modern government so far as it is a bureaucratic machine ; but it destroys rulership.

In effect, it leaves the state without a sovereign and, what is worse, without means to obtain one.

This is the greatest danger of a democracy, and it arises directly from the nature of liberty. Various attempts have been made to avoid it. The United States constitution, though devised for an opposite purpose, does give the President power to carry on the government in spite of opposition in Congress. The French President can dissolve the Chamber, but in practice he does not do it. Moreover, it would take days to get a new Chamber, and the emergency is usually a question of hours or minutes.

There is no permanent cure for a fault that arises from the nature of liberty itself, but it should be noticed that its danger is chiefly external. The internal strength of democracy is so great that it can stand not merely weeks but years of bad or weak government without collapse. No autarchy would have survived prohibition in the U.S.A. or the bank failures of 1933.

168. A weak or uncertain foreign policy has always been the chief danger of a democracy. It is rarely capable of decisive action in an emergency. Thus it may easily be destroyed by an attack from outside which it has perhaps expected but for which it has not prepared.

In this weakness democracy faithfully represents the people. The greater number of the people in any state take little interest in foreign policy and therefore do not trouble to know anything about it.

But education in foreign affairs would not prevent division of opinion. That belongs to temperament. The external danger to democracy will remain as long as the general condition of the world is that of anarchy. It is the common and inevitable danger of any peacefully disposed person living among savages and lunatics.

169. There are also economic dangers peculiar to democracy. Its organization cannot be planned as a whole. It is therefore both highly productive and extremely wasteful. The U.S.A. have the greatest production in the world, but waste more wealth in a year than would keep all the smaller states of Europe. In Britain there is also great waste.

Industrial strife, or competition for economic power, is another source of waste. It wastes not only the productive capacity of the workers but of the machines.

Both forms of waste can do injury in a democratic state which autarchies can avoid ; but both are set-off by great advantages.

The waste due to industrial competition is set-off by the increased fertility of production in a field open to creative liberty ; the waste due to strikes is set-off, or should be set-off, by greater liberty and greater prosperity in the workers.* That is to say, it secures for producers a rising market and for the whole state an increased stability.

170. The chief internal economic danger to democracy is not waste but disorganization.

This has its root, like a general deadlock, in the division of powers.   Two great unions in conflict can disorganize an industry ; all the unions in conflict with the state can produce, by a general strike, a general chaos.

171. Bankruptcy caused by any means, disorganization, strikes, war, is the chief internal danger of democracy.   It destroys the financial liberty of the people and therefore a great part of their independence.   Without funds they cannot strike ; they are at the mercy of any controlling power, and in practice they welcome any leader who will promise them renewed security of pay and work.   Hitler rode into power upon the slump.

172. Bankruptcy in a nation takes two forms : the collapse of its own currency ; the loss of real wealth.   The latter, which is the

* Where strikes are to be feared, employers raise wages as far as they can.   This, of course, is to their own advantage also in the long run.

147

only real bankruptcy, is rare. It occurs only when a nation squanders its natural resources without building up any compensating power of skill and organizing ability. For instance, an agricultural country which exhausts the fertility of the soil, destroys its forests, and loses its rainfall becomes a desert. It cannot support its people and they die out or emigrate. Such bankrupt territories are found in some parts of the world.

But the first form is the more common, and although it is not a real bankruptcy, and therefore not a total or permanent destruction of wealth, it produces the most dangerous form of disorganization in a state.

173. The failure of a currency may be due to inflation or mere panic. It always causes a direct loss of liberty to the state and the worker. The first loses freedom of financial action. It is driven by circumstances. The worker finds himself restricted by a new poverty.

The symptoms of inflation—rising prices, disorganized exchanges—are dreaded by all states. In autarchies laws are made forbidding prices to rise. But if the inflation is a true one, caused by an increase of money not balanced by production, the effect of such laws will only be to hide private ruin or suffering. They will also hide from the government the true state of its finances. Their final collapse is likely to be sudden and complete.

Rising prices, disorganized exchanges in a democracy are a useful symptom of danger to both government and people. It means that public confidence is disturbed or that the country is not paying its way.

174. The failure of a currency is not due, as many seem to think, to management. All currencies have always been managed. It is bad management that wrecks a currency.

A government that destroys its currency is likely to fall with it. For no loss of liberty is felt so immediately and sharply as money loss, especially by the poor. It presses upon them more hardly than the most tyrannical laws.

175. It is often said that all democracies commit suicide by one of two methods: either by reckless arrogance, like Athens, or by self-indulgence and moral degeneracy, like the Roman republic.

All these faults are imputed to all modern democracies by idealist critics. The arguments they urge are, for the first, interference with neighbours ; for the second, the emphasis laid by all radical and labour parties upon the rights of the people, and their silence about duties ; and the third, pacifism, egotism, atomism, and race-suicide.

The first charge, that democracies give offence by criticizing and threatening other nations, is true to this extent, that a free people, like a free man, is not afraid to express opinions, and that these opinions support freedom everywhere. Liberty as a real power is universal, real democracy knows no boundaries, and there is therefore a real common will of the world. If the peoples of the world could give their votes to-morrow, they would agree by an enormous majority on certain fundamental issues. They would demand a living wage, education, opportunity, security, leisure, and peace. This is the general will of the world, and every national democracy, simply because it is democratic, expresses it in its national form. The Frenchman has a different idea of opportunity and education, of the good life, from an Australian, but they use the same means to get them, democratic liberty.

The arrogance of any democracy laying down the law of the world is therefore the natural voice of liberty itself, common to the world. It is the same voice which speaks within a despotism or an anarchy, when leaders rise suddenly out of the mass to organize the power of the people for their security and advancement.

Where any democracy, then, by interference provokes enmity or involves itself in war, it is following its best nature ; and if it be destroyed, its end is like that of any great man who has fought for liberty and justice, honourable and glorious.

This is not abstract or romantic argument. Put it in this form : The majority of people in any democracy not corrupted by local vice or cowardice hate despotism and cruelty in any part of the world. It will therefore, if it has liberty of speech, protest against them. If this protest leads to war, the majority will suffer, many will die for their faith in goodness, in justice. These men are worthy of honour and so is the state that bred them.

176. The second charge against democracy is that it is selfish and founded in selfishness. This seems to contradict the first, but of course the word democracy is in this sense abstract. Democracy is people, and of a people a majority may be both interfering on some moral grounds and selfish in others. They may indulge their moral feelings by outcry against oppression, but refuse service to their nation when it faces the consequences.

In this case the moral act is still a good act. We all know the man of strong moral convictions who is at the same time completely selfish. Such men are often very pleased with themselves and quite unaware of their own selfishness. A great number of them, in all classes, cover it from their own eyes by some form of doctrine which absolves them from duty to the state. They say, "I'm not going to do anything for this government," or "If the country won't do so and so, I don't see that I owe anything to it."

These may be sincere beliefs. The test is the act of the person. For if he really believes that the state is not worthy of his support, and is an unselfish person, he will give time and effort to overturn the state. He will risk something, his skin or his job, to bring in that form of society which satisfies his moral will. This test in real life will divide the true men from the parasites.

But it is not true that a democracy breeds more parasites than autarchies. The difference is simply that in a democracy the parasite uses a different form of cover. He poses as a severely moral person, a stern critic, or sometimes as a pacifist. In an autarchy, the parasite, who is precisely the same type, self-indulgent, cowardly, or spoilt, grovels to the ruling power, finds new arguments to support tyranny, and grabs what he can of glory and profit with the least exertion.

But this difference, unreal in the individual, is real to the state. For the first type find their profit and security in refusing support to the state, taking the anarchist position ; the second in encouraging it in extreme absolutism.

Thus the first strengthens that tendency to disruption which is the inherent vice of all democracies ; the other increases the tendency to irresponsible violence which ruins all autarchies.

177. The atomism of democracy is a true danger, and it can be a vice. In so far as it is not the inevitable consequence of liberty and toleration, it is due to a false theory of the state. Modern democracies inherited the old theories of liberty, which lead inevitably to anarchy. These doctrines cannot change the real nature of liberty or the reality of a state. England, France, the U.S.A. are economic and cultural units, real organizations. But by teaching people false ideas about their relation to the state, by making them believe that their interests are necessarily opposed to all state action, they weaken their own cause and injure the power of the state.*

As soon as democratic liberty is seen by all classes to be the power which only organization can increase, trade disputes and political disputes tend to pass from the battle field into the council chamber. Since this is a real truth, since it is

---

* The violence of labour disputes in the U.S.A. is one product of this idea, grown upon the same ideal tree as Shakerism, etc.

the fact that organization increases liberty, we see wherever labour is organized under capable leaders that disputes tend to accommodation ; we see a tendency for employers and employed to meet together and say, "Our real interests are the same." But the atomism of the old thought still infects all those who either do not notice facts until they hit them in the face or do not check their political ideas with political realities.

178. Pacifism, regarded by absolutists as the chief vice of democracy, is not peculiar to it. All peoples hate war. The only war-seekers are found in certain youth movements, among neurotics, and among some abstract thinkers. Certain scientists, for instance, argue from the Darwinian theory that war is necessary to improve the race.

Pacifism is strong everywhere in proportion with real liberty. But it has in a democracy more direct influence upon policy.

179. Pacifism has three chief forms :

(1) Tolstoyan or non-resisting, accepting no state-made law.

(2) The doctrine of the man who says, "I accept the need of law and police, but not of armies or war."

(3) Of he who says, "Injustice and war are great evils. But they can only be restrained by good laws enforced by authority."

180. Tolstoy was logical. He denied the use of all force. Hinduism takes the same view, and some of their holy men may not kill even fleas or lice.

This form of pacifism rests, of course, on belief in a god or law controlling all men's acts. It denies liberty. It issues in anarchy or absolutism : for instance, the egotism of the fakir, the despotism of husband and ruler.

It denies also the reality of evil. But evil is real. A cancer which kills the young mother of a family is a real evil. A brute who cripples a child for life does real and irreparable evil. This is why non-resisting pacifism is considered heresy by the theologians.

181. In practice, non-resisters rarely take the logical position. They agree to restrain cruelty to children or animals. Their case then ceases to be defensible and they really ask, "How is evil to be overcome with the least possible violence ?"

They answer, "Love can overcome evil. Daily experience shows the power of forgiveness and sympathy."

182. Love truly overcomes evil. This is probably the most important truth of religion. But it does not overcome all evil, as religion itself insists. Hatred, intolerance, spite, greed— all these need the discipline of the will. In-

justice, disease, inequality of powers belong to the nature of reality and the perpetual conflict of good and evil within that nature.

183. The second type of pacifist, who accepts the violence of the law but rejects that of armed forces, is logically defenceless. He is, however, if not moved purely by some selfish fear, usually a man of political mind, deeply concerned with immediate policy. He is the propagandist, overstating his case.

184. These two classes, the anarchist and the sentimental or propagandist, have done immense good by attacking the nationalist and militant idea of the state. Most men hate war, but few give a life to fight against it. They are too busy. Tolstoy and his followers made the first effective assault upon the idol of imperial glory. But because they said "Trust love working as absolute ruler," and not " Trust love working in liberty by reason," they brought anarchy and confusion to Russia, instead of democracy.

185. Non-resisting or sentimental pacifism, since it has only emotional support, is subject to violent reversion. Serving soldiers in the last war can remember their surprise, when they came on leave, at the violence of former pacifists against the enemy. It was useless to tell them that Jerry in the German trenches was a man of

like feelings and anxieties with Tommy in the British.

186. Pacifism of the third class, of those prepared to use all available means, including force, to end war, is the commonest and the only rational. But it does not absolve men from using their own judgment to decide whether peace, in any given case, is better secured by concession or by force. Nothing can save them from this problem, because they are real men in a real world, and their liberty is also real. They cannot put it off from them.

187. Critics of democracy also contend that it leads to race-suicide and moral degeneracy.

A falling birth-rate is common to all modern states. It is the result of increasing liberty in people to control and organize their own lives.

Ambition for the children, ambition for self combine to limit the family. If democracies show a more rapid decline than autarchies, it is because they have succeeded better in giving liberty, education, and responsibility to the people.

188. A falling population is an evil in all states. It produces unemployment and defeatism. Although it is often the symptom of social health rather than degeneracy, it gives a nation the same sense of doom as belongs to a decaying family.

It produces even the doctrine that some mysterious cause forbids the intelligent to reproduce their kind. This notion is, of course, completely false.

189. Those who limit the family may do so from the highest motives : to give each child the best possible care and education. They cannot be accused of selfishness. Thus a fundamental problem of politics has been raised in an acute form. How far is any state justified in demanding children from parents, in securing its own future at the cost of living persons ? What can it answer to people who say, "Why should we consider the future condition of any state?" ?

The only possible answer by the state is this : "Because I stand for something—for traditions, ideals which are worth preserving."

190. The problem must be solved, of course, like all those raised by liberty, in liberty itself. The creative imagination will deal with its details as they arise. It is already beginning to see that having children is in itself a service to society and that the mother of a family carries an unequal burden.

Crèches, nursery schools, feeding of school-children should be made universal. All families with more than two children should have a rent allowance. Family tickets for all transport should be at reduced rates. A grant should be made to each mother for at least the first two years of a child's life, and her pension in old age should be proportioned to the number of her children. No doubt her children may wish to support her ; but what mother cares to be a burden on her children ?

191. A democratic state which fails to solve this problem will disappear and be replaced not by servile states or brave new worlds but by another form of the democratic state in which a different social plan will give women the power to realize their natural creative liberty without the artificial restraints which now prevent it.

The misery, boredom, and waste of kindness which we see everywhere, especially among women, is not the necessary product of liberty, but of anarchy and tyranny, of atomism, of egotistic thought and a bad social education.

192. In some parts of Africa, women possess already this liberty denied in European states. She can always, if she choose, marry and bear children. In many tribes, indeed, she is independent of a husband. The social idea does not revolve upon marriage, but upon blood relationship. A woman's kin come before the husband. Thus she will go home to bear her child, and stay at home perhaps two years.

Her husband has other wives meanwhile. Yet if a wife choose, she may cleave to her husband. Devoted couples are found in every village. Thus for women there is a choice of free action. She can be a mother and yet remain independent. Or she can give her energies to the new family.

193. Moral degeneracy and public corruption are imputed to democracy by every nationalist writer.

The truth is that a free press in a free country lives by criticism. Every newspaper likes to attack something or somebody, to discover some scandal, to show that the country is going to the dogs.

A foreign observer reading the English popular Sunday papers would say, "The English are a degenerate race in rapid decay." But, in fact, prisoners in gaols are 56,000 now against 180,000 in 1910. Crime is rapidly decreasing.

194. Public corruption is probably greater and much more dangerous, because less easily discovered, in autarchies than democracies. But in one special form it appears, at first sight, to belong only to democracy. Democratic statesmen are continually reproached or despised by idealist critics for suggesting a lie, or hiding behind some ambiguity.

This trickery has perplexed even democrats. It has produced in the free countries a great body of literature in which the politician is always a liar, traitor, and self-seeker.

* The truth is that democratic statesmen, as party leaders, are obliged to play the part of the advocate. No one finds fault with a barrister for making a good case on behalf of his client. A party leader is under the same duty. For he represents a group ; he is chosen to do so. Through him alone the group makes its will effective ; and if he fails to represent that will, he deprives it of its liberty. This fact is obvious to a parliamentarian. It puzzles only laymen. But it has been responsible for much sincere contempt, by foreign critics, of democratic institutions.

195. It is not true, therefore, that democracy necessarily produces a greater corruption or degeneracy than autarchy. Some democracies are corrupt and some autarchies. The real distinction is that democracies show the worst of themselves and autarchies the best, that the first are apt to be self-critical and the second complacent. Thus democracies continually expect ruin and survive a thousand catastrophes, whereas autarchies never expect it and crash at the first stumble.

* See *Democracy and the Organization of Political Parties*, Ostrogorski (translated by Clark), for a general account of the effect of real politics on the caucus orator. Macmillan, 1902.

196. The chief dangers of democracy, therefore, peculiar to itself, arise from division or conflict of powers. The results are not peculiar to any state. Bankruptcy within or conquest from without can befall them all. But democracies are more liable to financial panic and more hampered in their foreign policy than autarchies. In a world, therefore, still lawless, whose international relations are those of wild beasts which, when they suffer each other to live in peace, do so only because of fear, satiety, or whim, they resemble much more the stag and the buffalo, creatures formidable enough when attacked, but desiring only peace, than the lion and the eagle.

CHAPTER X

Democracy, International, Historical

197. International relations, like those of men, began in the assembly of masters, of the patriarchs. Europe in the Middle Ages was governed by the patriarchal kings, who consulted together—like the village elders of ancient Greece or modern Africa—to discuss and expound a law common to all, the law of the Roman church derived from the law of the empire. They twisted that law to suit themselves ; they attempted to defy it, like Henry II or John ; but they did not think of themselves as sovereigns. When they could see advantages in the law they appealed to it. The very idea of sovereignty as the fountain of positive law was unknown until the end of the sixteenth century, when Jean Bodin in France, after the rise of the nationalist sovereigns, expressed it in his book.*

Nationalism destroyed the law of Europe,

* *Six Livres de la République*, 1576.

defied the weak sanctions of the Pope, and brought anarchy. This was inevitable in the condition of the world at that time. Growing liberty and power in any nation or in any living creature is used to realize its strongest instincts according to its nature, and for that it requires independence. The man, when knowledge, wealth, or glory comes within his reach, is rebellious against all hindrance ; the nation, when it grows conscious of itself, defies authority. France, having driven out the English, very soon quarrelled with the Papacy and attempted to make it the servant of a nationalist France, in Avignon. The English nation had already, through Parliament, set national interest and pride before the claims of the Pope's delegate.

The Reformation was the rebellion of the free mind against a dogmatic theology. It expressed itself also in dogmatism, but it set up the standard of truth against the old crown of authority. It said, "To know truth for himself is a natural right of man," and therefore, even though it imagined all truth to lie in the Bible, it was the foster-parent of liberty.

But it was preceded by the nationalist revolt which had already broken up the old international law of Europe.

198. Nationalism is called the foremost and deadliest enemy of democracy. It has

caused more wars than religion or greed and it is the chief barrier to world democracy. It is the bitter enemy of truth, knowledge, of liberty and all its creative arts ; and the excuse for hatred and lies. Even in democratic countries children are still told lies about other nations in order to glorify their own. They are taught that their country is the noblest and their race the greatest in the world. These convictions are, of course, innate in the tribal instinct. A child is instinctively suspicious or fearful of strangers and attached to its own family and its own surroundings. Thus the nationalist doctrine, the idea based on the tribal or herd instinct, returns to strengthen instinctive force. Nationalist feeling increases by compound interest. The man who feels at the beginning that his own tribe is the greatest and grandest in the world delights in the idea of that greatness and grandeur when it is presented to him ; and then he loves the idea too and all its symbols.

Nationalist feeling destroys the free mind. It forbids a man to know any facts which deny the most ridiculous and worthless of creeds. I do not mean that love of country turns every man into a liar and makes a fool of him. All love their own land, but they need not therefore be blind to its faults and its crimes. Love has nothing to do with judgment. Perhaps the strongest love is in those who hate the faults because they love the good.

Nationalism stands not for this honest and fearless love of country, but for the self-deceiving passion which fears and hates truth.

199. It is often said that the idea of nationalism is artificial, an invented thing.

It is true that primitive races seem often to have little nationalism of feeling. They have not formed a national idea. British columns in Nigeria found no national resistance, and the foreign government was accepted by the people without resentment. They were much more interested in their family affairs, their private business than in the question of who was to rule them. So long as they were sure of security, justice, and liberty for their religions, they were indifferent to the race or colour of the governing power.

This is true of all peoples when the majority is poor. During the Napoleonic wars, French columns in Germany were better entertained by the people than their own troops. The poor everywhere find too much anxiety in the daily struggle for life to trouble their heads about a government which does nothing for them. They are usually indifferent patriots until the idea of nationalism is presented to them, and even then it often has small effect unless it is

joined to the idea of deprivation or of some
threat. If the poor are told "Foreign domination makes you poor" or "Foreign greed is
threatening to make you poorer," they are
naturally rebellious.

But this idea does not mean that the pure
nationalist idea, the passion for national glory,
with all its evils, was the chance invention of
some poet. The tribal instinct, family and
tribal feeling, is present in everyone, even the
poorest. The instinct for self-preservation may
thrust it into the background ; many people
have no time to think of anything but their
daily bread ; but it is perfectly certain that given
opportunity or leisure they will create a national
idea. To give people liberty of any kind,
economic, imaginative, but especially economic,
is to enable them to realize themselves and their
instincts, to know, to love, and to create. They
will realize their love of country in creating
the idea of its glory, and then they will seek to
realize that idea in fact.

The notion that a people which is beginning
to show nationalist feeling can be cured of it
by economic prosperity is absurd. Prosperity
makes liberty. It gives to people more power
in body and mind, more leisure to seek what
pleases them and to dream of glory. Men do
not strike or agitate in bad times when they are

poor and afraid, but in good when they have money, hope, and dreams. A subject people rebels when it begins to feel its strength. Thus the organization of an empire by a sovereign state, like the organization of a nation by a dictator, generates the power which will break up the empire and destroy dictatorship. This is inevitable because it arises from the nature of liberty itself.

200. Those who say that the liberal support of nationalism was foolish and wrong are thinking abstractly. Men of affairs like Palmerston, Gladstone, Campbell-Bannerman, dealing with real people and their passions, knew that the real folly was to defy or ignore a passion which roots in the strongest instinct of man and moves his deepest feeling. For a nationalist, patriotism unites the natural law which is the strongest emotion of the heart with religious devotion which is the passion of a soul. It is not for nothing that men speak of the mother country and give to their ideals the names of women. Even when they speak of the father-land, they give it a woman's name and worship it as a woman. Thus they die for her literally as lovers and as worshippers in a passion of devotion far greater and richer than anything known to lovers of real women, or to any but those few lovers of God whose mystical power

has been able to bring them the ecstasy of vision. Those who died for Greece, for Poland, for Ireland saw their darlings whenever they looked out of a window and knew her presence, more dear than that of a wife. They lived in her and she in them. Their delight was to serve her, and they looked to achieve greatness and triumph in laying down their lives for her. Love and the creative imagination of poets can do great evil and great good, but they are the very springs of man's life. To say to a man "You shall not love" is to say "You shall not live like a man, but like a machine." It is either useless or it destroys the man as a man.

Thus a practical statesman faced by this passionate love of country which threatens some danger does not say, "I will fight this love," but "I will use it for good if I can." His problem is not the abstract one—how to do the best thing—but the real one : how to make the best of a real situation.

The democratic answer in the nineteenth century was : Give the people their liberties and they will have no further reason for conflict; they will live at peace. This was too simple. It was founded on the old optimistic theory of human nature and of economics, of *laisser-faire*. It overlooked the vanity of peoples, which appears to be in direct proportion with their ignorance. It did not foresee the evil of nationalist rulers seeking to deceive a whole people in the interests of the nationalist religion, or that the devotion of patriots to their adored mistress could in the mass become a murderous passion to destroy everyone else who would not fall down before that idol. But the optimism of democrats does not alter the problem of its solution. The nations of the world, great and small, value their national liberty and will fight for it if they can. The national idea cannot be crushed out of a people even by centuries of oppression. Thus the real situation is not, How shall nationalism be abolished in a world society ? but, How shall separate nations, each with its own nationalist idea, be brought into a world democracy ?

201. Because liberty and democracy are real in the world as well as in the state, therefore the norm of greatest liberty applies throughout the world. It is the standard for world organization.

This fact is not seen because the anarchist and absolutist ideas which have been the enemies of liberty in state politics, but which are now gradually falling into contempt and weakness under the blows of real democracy, still have currency in world politics. They remain as ideas, and therefore they are always dangerous whenever facts do not stand in their way. They have wrecked in the world most of that primitive organization which, like the old semi-religious tribal laws, gave to the world before the war a standard of agreement.

The international organization of the world before the war was largely customary. It was founded on conscience and tradition ; its sanctions were the private honour or power of private people, either as individuals or firms. Even the gold standard, which was supposed in those times to be a self-regulating natural law comparable to the law of nature imagined by Proudhon, was in fact based upon custom, inertia, and convenience arising from the complexion of affairs at that time. Its real sanctions were not in any law of nature, but in the power of the international bankers controlling the distribution of credit.

Yet under this system, produced by the mere contrivance of humanity striving against the barriers of nationalism, a great devolution of wealth took place throughout the world. Remote and thinly populated countries, such as in primitive times remained for thousands of years under the oppression and limitations of deepest poverty, were able to acquire in forty or fifty years railways, roads, cities, a degree of public wealth which enabled them, when they chose, to undertake such public services as education.

This was a devolution of economic liberty which did not necessarily go far beyond the ruling sovereigns. It gave power to states and to small classes within the states, which they used often to assert themselves against their neighbours in wars of aggression and national glory. But no one pretends that the devolution of economic power by itself produces an ideal society. The point is not that the sovereign states of the world, rich and poor, even to the poorest, acquired some share of wealth under the old capitalistic international system of commerce ; but that humanity, as if by a private conspiracy, erected out of chaos, out of a tangle of civil war and obsolete nationalist economics, an international system for the common production and sharing of wealth. The production was unequal and the shares as between different classes and races were unjust, but both were accomplished in the teeth of national prejudice.

202. Merchants who found that the old mercantile law and the old tariffs were the enemies of prosperity, and economists in touch with them, invented the *laisser-faire* theory of trade. Adam Smith raised the common experience of trade into an abstract philosophy.

He said, in short : "All state regulation of trade or conditions of work is bad.   All the economic evils which we see, such as poverty and waste, are the consequences of state interference."   It was the anarchist theory of economics.   It presumed, like all anarchist theory, that there was a self-regulating economic principle in nature which, left to operate by itself, would produce wealth for everybody.

Just as anarchists like Rousseau and Tolstoy, fighting bad states, did great good, because they had more truth and goodness than the states, so the economic anarchists, by destroying bad and oppressive laws and purely obstructive tariffs, brought prosperity to the world.

Its great merit, like that of all the anarchist theories, was that it gave a rule for all mankind. It treated world society as the only real society, and regarded national boundaries as artificial barriers.

Its fault, as in all theory founded in the idea of automatic process or law, was to mistake the nature of man and his relation with society. It treated him as an economic unit completely independent and at the same time determined by economic law.   Thus it gave the manu-facturers the right to act as dictators to their workers and as anarchists in society.   It ignored the social relations of a worker, and presumed

173

that he could follow employment wherever it was to be found at the centre of cheapest production.

The free-trade theory, like that of liberty, expressed in a positive form, is not *laisser-faire*, but the greatest power of production and exchange to the greatest number of states.

Thus any measure which promotes international trade is good, and any tariff which is meant to injure that trade is an injury to world production and world society, and therefore to states and men.

A nation that refuses to trade with others or attempts to make itself self-sufficient takes the same position as an individual who attempts to withdraw his capital or labour from the use of society.

203. The action of real democratic power in the world before the war made prosperity in spite of national barriers, and even destroyed the barriers. But just as the anarchists like Bakunin and Kropotkin, since they found all men good, imputed all evil to the organization of the state and especially to its economic system, so anarchist thinkers now say to separate states, "You are a sovereign individual owing allegiance to none. You can therefore repudiate all obligations, all treaties, all debts."

Just as dictators like Hitler are at once

anarchists and absolutists, saying, "My will is the only law ; therefore I can break all other laws and the world shall obey my will alone," so all states that acknowledge no higher law than their own will and convenience are enemies of liberty.

They are therefore enemies of their own security and prosperity, which depend upon the economic organization of the world. Capitalism in the world, as in the state, is not good or bad in itself ; it is simply a necessity. Moreover, between states it is always private capitalism, for even if a state like Russia holds all capital, it deals with the world like a single financier or manufacturer.* Its economic relation with governments or firms is that of a private individual. A state that dishonours its obligations is exactly in the same position as a private person, does the same injury to public credit, and suffers the same damage to its own.

This discovery is quickly made by all states which, nursed on anarchist theory, are eager to repudiate ; and each almost at once finds itself trying to escape the consequences, to organize a new system of international credits in place of the old.

204. As men and states are both judged by the norm of the greatest liberty—by education,

* The Soviet Government has, of course, been careful to honour its own foreign obligations.

leisure, standards of living, and political integrity —so nations themselves as individuals in the world democracy should be judged by the amount of liberty which they give to the common stock. Thus it could be said of a nation, as of a man, that it had made good use of powers which belonged to it by nature, but it had shirked its public duty. It was parasitic on the world society.

Nations are already judged by this norm. We read every day of the debt owed by civilization to the Greeks or the Romans, to the religious genius of the Jews, the arts of Italy, German music, French painting. It is only because world democracy is in a still more primitive state than national democracy and because the very ideas of liberty and democracy are confused that the organization of international trade, banking, and transport is not seen to be equally an important service to the world and to liberty.

To organize a state for production is always to increase real if not actual democracy ; to secure peace and the devolution of capital throughout the world, by any means, tends inexorably towards world democracy and the world state.

Many who look back sadly to the world before the war think that liberty has been lost to it.

But that world resembled the primitive age of the patriarchs, golden in legends, but in fact oppressive and unstable. It glittered only on the surface. Its organization was not founded in the reality of man's liberty, but in a lucky and temporary balance of forces. Its faith was in jujus like the automatic gold standard, and mystery religions like the dialectic. Its security was delusive. At sea it was maintained only by the British fleet taking care of its own imperial interests. In trade it depended on a few international bankers taking care of their common interests. On land it did not exist. Every diplomat in Europe knew that war was certain and that it would break that sparkling dream into pieces. It was only because people had no idea of their danger that it did not trouble them. Now that the old traditional organization is broken up, they think that the world is going backwards. But the fact is only that the old dangers are seen, the old oppressions are noticed, and that the bombing plane has brought for the first time to the imagination of the whole peoples the meaning of war. It is not true, as some say, that the world has gone mad. It has been wakened from a dream, from the hallucinations of a progress founded on luck ; and it is now much less ignorant and blind than it ever was before. It can no longer

177

ignore facts when they fly in the air at two hundred miles an hour with five-hundred-pound bombs. Thus the world is nearer real security now than it was thirty years ago. For it is beginning to understand its own nature, the nature of its problem, and the means of peace. It is beginning to see that world security is exactly the same kind of problem, on a larger scale, as public security within a state, and that the same means must be used to get it, the establishment of a real law sovereign over the world.

205. It was the nearness of the patriarchs which made their quarrels into the bitter and dangerous feuds of near neighbours, able at any moment to destroy one another. It brought war to their doors and obliged them to make agreement and to form at last the state sovereign over private quarrels.

It is the nearness of sovereign states which brings them first into war and then forces them into understanding. As transport grows quicker, the need of agreement is more urgent. During the nineteenth century Britain still stood apart from Europe. Now Britain is tied to Europe by many agreements, public, private, or tacit, and is extremely anxious to find some solid ground for a general agreement.

But the U.S.A., since they are still at some

distance from Europe and Japan by the quickest transport, do not want to join in any binding agreements. Their best interest, as they see it, is to stand aside. When the further improvement of the aeroplane, in which they themselves are foremost, has brought them within easy bombing radius of the enemy, they too will enter into agreements and alliances, public, private, or tacit, with other nations for their own security.

206. Since each man is both an individual and a member of society, he seeks power in competition and co-operation. Throughout history, therefore, he has fought and traded at the same time. African tribes which were at perpetual war nevertheless had trade agreements. They exchanged certain products which each needed, and gave safe passage to merchants providing both.

Throughout history during nationalist wars and religious wars there has always been trade and travel.* Men were always ready to risk their lives for the wealth which would enable them to satisfy their instincts or realize their ideas. The reckless enterprise of men in pursuit of wealth and learning, of all kinds of achievement, battled with the obstacles, set up nationa-

* For its extent and importance to-day, as a movement of international liberty among nationalist quarrels, see *The Tourist Movement* : Ogilvie. King, 1933.

list fears and passions, nationalist finance and its mercantile system, the primitive suspicion and conceit natural to tribes cut off from variety of ideas and the comparison of arts.

It penetrated even in the Middle Ages to China and India by journeys measured in years, and sailed blind through Atlantic and Pacific in boats smaller than a Thames barge.

Political liberty since the fall of the Athenian and Roman empires was small, but liberty of education, manufacture, knowledge, and travel grew steadily. The new ships of the fifteenth century enlarged man in the whole world ; the inventions, products, and arts of every people made openings for the imagination and enjoyment of the rest.

207. Trade, like nearness, led to agreement, but of a different kind. Near neighbours for their own sakes formed alliances for defence or conquest. The history of every part of Europe, for instance of the Italian states, recorded by Machiavelli, shows a mass of bargaining and treaty making. Each prince or president tried to obtain allies by some binding agreement, secured by marriage or fear, and to undermine his enemies. What then occupied Italy now occupies the world.

But trade agreements, secured by natural advantage, had much more stability. The element of co-operation was there stronger than that of competition.

Instruments of credit, revived in the thirteenth century, had no sanction but common interest. But this interest belonged to all men, whatever their language, race, or religion. It was above nationalism ; a Catholic merchant in Venice honoured the drafts of a Mahometan in Turkey or a Parsee fire-worshipper in Persia, not because any treaty existed between them or any court had jurisdiction over them, but because it paid him to do so. His honour was a commercial asset.

Thus gradually, as trade increased with new inventions and better transport, the world became a network of commercial obligations.

Nations discovered at last the advantages of co-operation and the old nationalist mercantile systems broke up. Alliances and treaties were composed for trade as well as peace or war.

208. The natural creative power of world democracy produced even the rudimentary organs of a world state : a postal union organizing mails for the world, and international standards of time, measure, weight, and currency * ; a central news service, insurance and maritime service. All this was accomplished

* The International Bureau of Weights and Measures, at Paris, dates from 1875 ; of time, however, only from 1919.

by liberty itself, without any agreed plan, without any theory, in the teeth of nationalist ignorance and selfishness.

The international system developed by the experience of merchants accustomed to think in terms of the world instead of the state was so like a world law that many thought of it as a kind of natural law, based on the gold standard.

It supplemented those diplomatic agreements between nations which sought to regulate war and treaty making, which produced the world court of international justice at The Hague and the great body of international regulations called International Law.

CHAPTER XI

Democracy, International, Organization

209. John Austin * defined law as the fiat of a sovereign. International lawyers do not like a definition which declares that their law is not law—since no sovereign exists to enforce it—and that they have no right to their title. They argue that international law is enforced every day. For instance, at this moment it is quoted for support by both sides in the King's Bench, where the King of Italy is suing the Emperor of Abyssinia for a sum of money. Thus international laws have real legal effect when they are used in national courts. They have such effect daily in courts of admiralty.

But until the foundation of the League of Nations there was no power capable of enforcing them between sovereigns in the international field.

International law was only real law when it ceased to be international.

210. Definitions have no value unless they

* 1790–1859. Professor of Jurisprudence, London.

convey a real truth, a real distinction. Austin's definition had this value because it confined the name of law to rules which had to be obeyed, and that is exactly what men want to know about them and what gives them use. Attempts to find in law a moral sanction lead to confusion. No doubt all law is an expression to some extent of moral ideas common to humanity, and it is obeyed not solely because of its threat but partly for justice. Men do not refrain from murder only because they are afraid of hanging. But the vigilance committee with its rope has stopped murder and brought comparative peace to numberless mining-camps, and this was the important fact for the peaceful majority. A new-comer to such a camp did not want to know whether moral ideas existed there, but whether there was a sheriff and a force capable of enforcing law. Moral ideas exist wherever men are, and there is more goodness and good nature in every community than strife ; but one bully, one lunatic fool or drunken brute will abolish their effect.

International law breaks down exactly at this point, where some nation decides to act the bully or the brute. But since it has the name of law and since it has actual legal effect in national courts, it would be pedantic to refuse it the name. It is better to give another name to the true law which could be enforced between nations and call it supernational.*

211. The first measure of true supernational law was the covenant of the League of Nations. It was a true law because it was enforced by a sovereign : the League council had authority to punish aggressors by blockade. They could be ruined, if necessary, by the destruction of their commerce.

The League failed to secure world peace because the U.S.A., most powerful of existing states, refused to join it and because the great powers which were members brought to the council chamber the same jealousies and fears which had always divided them. They could agree to coerce some weaker state, but they could not allow themselves to be treated as subjects.

Many think that these faults will always make a sovereign league impossible. They cannot imagine great states submitting themselves to judgment. But anyone who reads the history of an actual League conference, for example the Disarmament Conference, will see how nearly all states did come to agreement, and how often they were persuaded to take risks and to make concessions for agreement.†

* I believe Madariaga, in his book *The World's Design*, 1935, first used this word. The book is excellent upon international relations and the League.
† See *The Whispering Gallery of Europe*, Temperley. Collins, 1938

212. The truth is that all argument against the League founded on the notion of an inevitable conflict between sovereigns is abstract, the product of a study table. The real situation is more complex. Since world society and the interdependence of nations is a real thing, that is to say, since world democracy exists already as the ground of all power, nations most bitterly opposed in idea find themselves compelled by facts to agree together. They storm against each other in the press and privately seek credits or bargain for trade. They do so only because they must ; because they have to provide for their peoples, whose interests all over the world are the same.

213. The world state is certain because the same forces that made the national state are at work to bring it forth. It can come in the same way, by two routes or by any combination of them. As a state autarchy arose from the decay of patriarchs, so a world autarchy could come from the fall of the existing democracies, either by some inherent weakness or a refusal to defend themselves, before a single conqueror or gang.

Its history would then resemble that of national states under tyrants, such as the Russian, Austrian, Roman, British, or German empires : federation of powers, improvement of transport, coding of law, increased production of wealth, accompanied either by devolution of responsible government, such as transformed the British empire, or by increasing stupidity, jealousy, cynicism, and corruption among the ruling caste or party, such as almost destroyed that empire in the eighteenth century.

The world empire would be changed into world democracy either by peaceful devolution or through a series of revolutions and counter-revolutions.

But this route is unlikely. The only powers which dream of world conquest are weak and divided. They are competitive by nature and therefore they cannot trust one another.

It is more probable that the world state will arise, like the village assembly, from conference and agreement among the masters. That agreement was forced upon the scattered patriarchal families by their closeness. A war now between any two European peoples could start without sign or notice and begin the destruction of great cities within five or ten minutes. Europe is like a Wild West camp where every man carries a loaded gun, where no law stops any drunken fool or brute from doing murder. But no frontier camp endured murder and insecurity for very long. The roughest was often the first to set up its vigilance committee and to hang the public nuisance.

Europe's first vigilance committee failed for lack of support, and the nations have now fallen back into anarchy. But the very fact that every nation is armed and desperate brings a final peace nearer.

214. This does not mean that world peace can come only through an international authority with its own police force. It took a thousand years even in England to set up an efficient police force. An international police force would be still harder to contrive. Suppose its weapon were the bombing plane. What Briton, German, Frenchman, or Italian is going to take responsibility for blowing up the factories and bridges in his own country ? In practice, the executive committee would be divided by every national dispute and the situation would be the same as before, a group of peace-desiring peoples against war-makers.

215. There is very little chance that the peace-desiring peoples will combine. The most powerful of them, the U.S.A., is still convinced of its own security in isolation. Its sympathies are divided, very much as those of England were divided sixty years ago, between France and Germany. Its people are still in the vast majority suspicious of all foreigners,

and in idea, like their English counterparts of sixty years ago, hostile to all government organization, internally and externally. That suspicion, natural in a people of free church tradition, destroyed the old League and would certainly reject another.

But formal agreement between the patriarchs was not brought about by mere good will. It was forced upon them by necessity, by the selfish desire to save themselves, to gain themselves some benefit. In the same way, nations are brought to act together by a common advantage. It is this fear, this necessity, operating simply upon the fears of governments, which has already forced British conservatives to confer with Russian communists and the U.S.A. to come to a tacit understanding with the British Admiralty. Without alliance or agreement, without any common understanding or sympathy between peoples, events still force the peace-desiring into co-operation against a group of war-makers.

216. If President Wilson had not set up the League, it would still have been invented by some other.* It was a necessary development of history.

But the Geneva League has had the same effect upon world history as the constitution of Solon

* But, as Madariaga says, "Wilson's greatest merit is that he would not wait" : *The World's Design*, p. 22.

189

and Cleisthenes on national history. Their first democratic state revealed to all peoples the possibility of something which they had formerly dreamed ; or not even dreamed, but only needed. It therefore enormously increased man's power to achieve a political democracy. For he saw what he wanted and he knew that it could be got.

So when the Versailles Treaty and the covenant of the League gave to world society the first constitution founded on the equality and power of the masters, all men saw a dream realized and formed a concrete ambition.

Millions who know nothing of the League, or think of it as a failure, have clearly in their minds this knowledge, that humanity once set up for itself a constitution for the world.

The idea of such a constitution will be realized in a new league, by the continuous pressure of the common need and desire, as inevitably as the democratic constitutions of the national state.

217. It is often said that war would destroy civilization. The argument is, "The dictators, if we do not give way to them, will fight and the world will be ruined. Therefore, let us give way to them now and save what we can."

This is false. War would destroy the dictators, but not civilization.

218. The reason is that industrial skill and

scientific knowledge cannot be destroyed. Factories can be blown to pieces, but the knowledge to organize them remains. A ruined world, to modern men of power, would not be chaos but opportunity.

The last war did not throw back the advancing power of liberty, but greatly increased it. Much political disorder since the war has been due simply to the rapidity of that advance, the sudden leap in the experience of millions from the old world of caste, of traditional loyalties, into new freedom, new standards of life, high wages, and individual independence.

Those who saw what government organization could do in feeding, housing, and clothing whole populations during the war asked, fairly : Why can it not do the same work, to better advantage, in peace ? Thus arose not only the exaggerated hopes of the communist but all those schemes for making wealth out of paper money which have since confused the real problem of distributing the new wealth. But with all the confusion, there is both more wealth and a higher standard of living, of education, among all the democracies. There is more liberty.

CHAPTER XII

Education for Liberty, General

219. A child is formed by a total experience which begins as soon as it can use its will or form an idea. It learns at first from its parents, toys, friends, any accident or illness that may befall it. It learns from its total environment, which, as it grows up, gradually includes the ideas of the time, daily history as related in the press, books, public ceremonial, and finally the exercise of its political rights and duties. The experience cannot be separated into ideal and real ; what is grasped in idea is tested in action. But since the idea precedes the act and falls more directly under the control of those agencies called educative, it is more easily treated under a separate head.

220. Education is that part of a child's total experience which is arranged for specific purposes. It is controlled experience. It consists of instruction at home or at school ; games meant to develop muscle or character ; visits to

farms, factories, plays, the cinema ; reading chosen to give a certain knowledge or sensation.

221. A total environment is partly real, partly spiritual or ideal. Religion, national tradition, current opinion and taste, the press form a spiritual environment more compelling in effect than physical surroundings. The difference between nations is chiefly a difference of the ideal environment. It is more influential than race. As between the free states and the bound, the chief part of the difference, entering into all facts, is the standard of toleration.

222. Toleration is the natural air of freedom. Without it there is full liberty only for one man, one opinion, one party, or one creed. Whatever means a state uses to repress or limit the free production and exchange of ideas are destructive of liberty. For as ideas demand action, a man who acquires no new ideas initiates nothing and adds nothing to the power, knowledge, and liberty of society.

This does not mean that his action is not creative. All his actions originate novelty. But if he merely obeys an order or repeats a lesson, what he brings new into the world is merely a repetition. Workmen who build a car make something new, but it is the same as thousands of the old. A child who repeats a poem creates of symbols on the page a new experience for himself and others, but not a new poem.

A scientist who taught only what he had been taught would add nothing to science, and if all scientists believed that their science was complete, that nothing new was to be learnt, scientific inquiry would come to an end. There would be no new discoveries or new inventions.

A mind closed to new truth has been called dogmatic. Such minds, having rejected freedom for themselves, always try to deny it to others. They become the enemies of all truth so far as it stands upon facts.

223. Dogma has two meanings. At first it meant only a declared belief.* In this sense all men and all churches are dogmatic. Cardinal Newman is thinking of this use when he writes of his early faith and the principles on which it was based :

"First was the principle of dogma ; by liberalism I mean the anti-dogmatic principle. . . . from the age of fifteen dogma has been the fundamental principle of my religion. I know no other religion. . . . as well can there be filial love without the fact of a father as devotion without the fact of a Supreme Being." †

* This book, for instance, which having defined a belief affords a clear and distinct target for shooters.
† *Apologia pro Vita Sua*, Chap. II.

194

Newman means that a man who cannot believe in a real god cannot have a religion.

But the second and more usual meaning of dogma is belief enforced by authority. This arises out of the first because a man who forms a belief is very apt to think that it is the only true and right one. So Newman, the gentlest of men, writes about certain leaders of heresy :

"The latter should meet with no mercy . . . to spare him is a false and dangerous pity. It is to endanger the souls of thousands."

Newman's idea is now that there is only one truth in the world about religion, which he knows, and that anyone who attacks that truth or denies it ought to be silenced.

224. Everyone, whether cardinal or scientist, who believes that his own truth is complete and final must become a dogmatist of this kind. The more sincere his faith, the more he is bound to persecute, to save others from falling into error. But the dogmatists of history, both in science and the churches, are continually overwhelmed by new facts. The scientists are forgotten and the churches either disappear or silently change their creeds.

225. Since truth is not complete, men must have power to seek and publish what they think to be the truth. Progress is impossible without toleration.

The idea of toleration was known for a long time before Locke wrote his book,* but there is little more of the practice now than in 1690. Even in democratic states where all religions are protected, there is racial and political intolerance. The principle itself, even when it is used, is often misunderstood. People state it thus : "Toleration is the only way to peace, because it is impossible to make people change their habits and opinions."

But this is a wrong and dangerous doctrine, because it is untrue and also because it denies the moral responsibility in man. It is false that letting people alone is the only way to peace. It is often the shortest cut to war and cruelty. It would abolish all such societies as the Aborigines Protection Society or societies for the prevention of cruelty. Thus, like other false ideas, it is a direct challenge to man's love of truth and power combined, for by attacking it he can satisfy both. But also it denies man's responsibility for others, for his dependents and finally for society. It is on this ground that so many great and noble-minded men have rejected it with contempt. They say, "Are we to allow children to be done to death in mines and factories in order to avoid trouble and abuse for ourselves ?" No honest man believes in tolera-

* *Letter of Toleration*, 1685.

196

tion when it is grounded in cowardice and selfishness.

226. But since the search of truth involves not only the use of power given by society but conflict, toleration itself cannot be merely abstract and permissive. The battles of religion, for instance, between Hindu and Mahometan, must be tolerated by the state, but this idea does not mean that the state ought to stand aside from the quarrel. The state has a duty to protect both sides, to save each from the oppression of the other. It must secure to each, as far as possible, the liberty of expressing religious opinion and practising the religious life.

227. The intervention of the state is only justified to prevent violence on some actual occasion. For instance, it has no right to suppress some party or sect because it happens to excite popular hatred and so to produce a continual threat of violence. Every new sect and religion in the world, especially the Christian religion at its beginning, has been a danger to public peace and has been denounced with the same violence.

228. It is sometimes said that toleration should be refused to the intolerant. In practice this would destroy it. All men of strong opinions incline to intolerance; many great artists, scientists, philosophers, and saints have

197

been ferocious enemies of all ideas except their own. The same rule therefore applies to the intolerant as to the rest ; they must have as much liberty to express themselves, to preach and to abuse other preachers, as the state can secure to them. If they procure violence or danger to the general liberty, they can be restricted, but only so far as it is necessary to prevent violence at a specific time and place.

229. Toleration as the ground of freedom is itself a truth, expressed in this form : "Because final truth is not known and can never be complete, all expressions of it have equal title to be heard."

230. Men are by nature intolerant and in practice all are dogmatic. Some may have more truth in their belief, some more falsehood ; but they must believe something and that they will teach. A democratic country differs from an autarchy only in this, that it has a hundred dogmatic religions and political creeds instead of one.

This is its strength, the seed of its fertility and the virtue of its being. For it means not only the endless experiment of new ideas and the cross-fertilization of minds, which have given to all democracies the richness of their invention, but the fitting to each mind of its proper means of realization.

Newman in England became a Roman Catholic because from the beginning his nature inclined him to that faith. Thus he, who had arrived at dogmatism and was willing to force belief on others, did not suffer himself from an enforced belief. He enjoyed the virtue of liberty in refusing to believe anything except by his own will. Thus he achieved himself in his unique quality of greatness.

231. It is often noticed that converts to a religion are more fervent than the old faithful. But this follows from their case. They become converts only because their nature demands that religion.

If Newman had been born in Calvin's Geneva and forced into the Calvinist faith, he would have been cramped and spoiled. Suppose Bunyan had been born in Italy or William Blake in Spain ; the first would have been a monk and the second would have been imprisoned. In both cases genius would have been sterile and the world deprived.

This does not mean that religion is or ought to be a matter of taste, but only that it should engage the whole nature of the man. The standard of the religious society is the greatest spiritual achievement of the greatest number, the highest perfection of men each in his own character ; and sincerity is the ground of character. Religious liberty, like political liberty, is therefore essential to man's achievement.

232. The dogmatist in a free country, where truth is sought and published, must defend his principles. They stand beside all the rest to be judged, and if they are weak or false they are likely to be exploded. It is often said that a false creed cannot be destroyed except by the death of believers ; that nobody ever changes his mind about an ultimate faith, whether in religion, politics, or some science. This is perhaps true, but in a democracy the creeds themselves, if they are false or shallow, die very quickly, because young people, before they are committed to them, can learn their weakness or find some better belief.

233. Truth is not stronger than falsehood. A well-directed lie can overwhelm it. Truth is not designed for any special purpose, to be impregnable or attractive ; and lies are like weapons, invented only to kill. The reason why any truth is not finally destroyed by lies is because, if it is really true, it is in the nature of things, and however often it is beaten down and crushed out of sight, it will be found again.

Lies are universal. Greater power of expression in democracies probably increases both the number and the force of the lies which continually bombard each other and the truth. But the force of democratic liberty is that the search for truth is not prevented, so that it is continually being rediscovered, restated, and purified.*

234. The only remedy for dogmatism and lies is toleration and the greatest possible liberty of expression. All general censorship, whether of books or press, is in itself bad, because it may prevent truth or destroy original art. It actually does so every day.

By general censorship I mean the forbidding of publications by general rule—for instance, all opinions classed as obscene or all opinions classed as seditious. This is the equivalent of suppressing a political party or a sect by force. The rule of political toleration should be that processions or meetings can only be forbidden by special warrant at a specific time and place in order to avoid violence actually threatened. The rule of censorship should be that the sale or display of books or papers can only be forbidden in specific places where actual injury can be feared. That is to say, all publication, except of criminal libel, should be allowed, but the display for sale where it might offend religious or moral prejudice could be restricted. No art

* Professor Laski gives two necessary conditions for political liberty : (1) education to express wants intelligibly ; (2) provision of honest views : *Grammar of Politics*. Allen and Unwin.

exhibition in a gallery could be censored, and if it offended susceptibilities of any kind it would have the right to protection ; but leave to show statues or pictures in any open place would depend on the local standards of taste and morals.

The same rule should apply to plays. Absolute liberty should belong to the theatre, within an amended law of libel. A visitor to the theatre who chanced unexpectedly to be shocked would be in the same position as any private citizen who is disgusted or offended in the ordinary course of things. He cannot ask, as many do, what the censor is doing. This is to think and speak like an absolutist or an anarchist—the man who assumes that what he feels and thinks should be a universal law.

235. This is the common view because of man's natural dogmatism. As Mill pointed out, if censorship were designed to please everybody, it would forbid everything : every art, every form of scientific inquiry, every kind of enjoyment, all religions and all political parties. Everything has been forbidden at some time. At the present moment there are powerful groups in England who would like to abolish the English church, the Roman Catholic church, all the other churches, the imperialist party, the fascists, the communists ; they propose to drive the Scots out of England, the

English out of Wales, the Irish out of Scotland, Jews out of everywhere ; they wish to suppress the doctors, the herbalists, the bonesetters ; they would stop publication in newspapers of trials, inquests, financial advertisements, medical advertisements.

We are all convinced that certain opinions, tastes, amusements, or books are dangerous and worthless. We may be right, but in history far wiser men have been wrong. This does not mean that we can sit back in a false toleration of what we think evil, but that from the conflict of ideas there is no escape in censorship. Each must fight for his creed and let history decide the issue.

The ideal in any state is the abolition of all censorship, for even now it is not needed in private life among people of ordinary manners and education. Everything can be read, said, or discussed without offence.

236. The support of censorship is always stronger in the provinces than in a capital, and in backward countries than in those more advanced, because in provincial towns or backward countries the people have a narrower experience of life and their local leaders are more self-satisfied.

It is not true that townsmen are cleverer than country folk or that Londoners are better educated than the Midlander, or even that they read more ; but they hear more opinions and they are accustomed by experience to a greater liberty. They realize by experience, which is often the substitute for imagination, how much liberty of expression and variety of opinion can be allowed without the smallest injury to public peace or morals. Half an hour in Hyde Park among the speakers or Tottenham Court Road among the book-shops would be better education for the provincial statesman or councillor and his censors than years of scholastic instruction.

237. A more reasoned demand for censorship comes from those who think that the public taste is being destroyed by bad films and books.

But, in the first place, censors do not attack bad art. They are not concerned with art, but with politics, as in Germany and South Africa, or religion, as in Spain or Eire. When they judge of taste they are always wrong.

All states and churches, like the academies, show to the world an endless chain of follies and defeats. The name of every great religious genius, of every great scientist, artist, and musician is a reminder of official conceit, ignorance, spite, and final ignominy.

But apart from the historical imbecility of censorship, it is not true that standards of taste are worsening. Vast new populations which recently were almost illiterate now demand reading and art. But since their education stops at fourteen, their favourite plots are like folk-lore and they look in their papers for the story that delighted the ballad singers—murder and adultery.

Meanwhile the class which formerly enjoyed what was called the aristocratic culture is now ten times greater and more widely cultivated than ever before. Books, plays, pictures of the front rank have never enjoyed so quick and wide an appreciation.

238. Liberty of the press is not only a social right but the chief security of a state. No secret services in the world can tell a ruler so much about the real feelings and opinions of the ruled as an independent press. The dictators even now seek their news of democratic feeling in the free press.

239. The reason is that popular feeling is far too complex and shifting for judgment by the secret agent, even if he is honest and un-prejudiced. It resembles the weather. It can be gauged only by men of experience dealing with the greatest possible variety of given facts. Now, in an independent press these facts are still selected by prejudice, but by prejudice representing all shades of opinion which are themselves known, so that they can be allowed

205

for. The official agent, even when he is competent, is a mystery, because his character is official. It is his uniform. The reporter is known by his opinions and his newspaper ; his character is known and can be judged.

But, in fact, official agents, especially when they are secret agents, are usually bad. How often they write from their imagination to save the trouble of research which cannot be checked, how commonly they report not the truth even as they conceive it, but what they think will please, is known to everyone who has had to use them.

240. The most insidious form of censorship in many countries is the libel law. In England it is especially bad and dangerous. It is used to blackmail newspapers and writers, whose counsel tell them that however good their case, even in law, they would be wise to pay anything in reason to avoid an action.

Libel must be checked and punished. False or malicious publication can do great wrong. In France lately Salengro, a cabinet minister, was driven to suicide by lies. The French law is too weak. Malice and especially malicious falsehood should be heavily punished. But malice should be proved. Repetition is a strong proof of malice, and should be absolutely prevented.

A libel law is necessary. But to give a man right of action and heavy damages when all the damage he can prove is a hypothetical injury to his character is to invite the blackmailer, and to lay the most oppressive and stupid censorship on the press and on all publications.

241. It is the great danger of such censorship, either indirect through a bad libel law or direct through the common law, that its effects are not seen. They are deprivations, and nobody knows what he has lost if he has never had it. A people which has never known a free press does not miss it. It suffers in judgment, security, knowledge, in a thousand ways ; but it does not realize it, and if revolution befall it looks upon its misfortunes as an act of God.

Anybody who wants to know the injury done year after year in the most unexpected quarters by the British laws of censorship and libel should ask editors and writers, the B.B.C., even scientists, how much they are affected by it. It appears like a trifle to the public, but it affects the public in every part of its experience ; it gives a certain force to its news, it cuts out certain facts, it prevents the discovery of corruption, it hides a public scandal, it is a continuous danger to liberty.

242. Censorship is sometimes defended on the grounds that children may take harm from

newspaper reports of sexual offences, from obscene books, or from unorthodox opinion.

But children take harm from no truth or candour ; only from confusion and mystery.

In which household does a child most quickly learn the true worth and scale of things, the distinction between love and lust, between modesty and shame, between sincerity and hypocrisy, truth and cowardice—one in which he can discuss anything, read everything, and in which he knows that truth will always be sought ; or one in which his questions meet evasion, snubs, or a dogmatic ruling, "This is right and no question about it" ?

Doctors tell us every day that from the second class come all the neurotics, perverts and many, perhaps all, of those criminals who act upon impulse : the stranglers of children, kleptomaniacs, pyromaniacs, maimers, sadists—creatures who puzzle every jury with the question, Are they more mad or wicked ?

243. But if freedom is good for children, why is it bad for a nation ? Why should grown people be prevented from seeing and reading everything that is offered ? The usual answer is that offence would be given to the public's sense of decency or to special groups and sections of the public.

244. This objection, which in actual

politics is the driving force of censorship, is a special case of the first. The public were children once, and as children they were educated either for liberty or for servility and cowardice.

245. The only criterion for lawmakers is, therefore : What is the quickest way to liberty, without risk to its existing framework ? Children should be educated in freedom and every means taken to cut down censorship. Freedom of mind, the courage to know and to learn, is the only foundation of self-respect and responsibility.

246. Propaganda has been used since the war with an effect astonishing to the old-fashioned optimist. Men of distinction and importance solemnly repeat the stuff which was invented to deceive nazi hooligans or fascist school-children.

This is not cause for despair but energy. It is simply another proof of what should have been obvious long ago—that the comparative peace and decency of the century between Waterloo and Liége * were not due to any real force or depth of world civilization, but to luck. Governments did not glory then in the torture and murder of minorities only because they had not discovered how easy and profitable it could

* A century when Armenians, Jews, and Red Indians were hunted down like beasts ; but not by ideal and consistent policy.

be. They kept treaties and obligations not because they had no will to break them, but because they did not dare or it did not pay.

Propaganda, like the bombing plane, is a deadly enemy of liberty, but democracy had and has no security until it is proof against them both, for they were bound to be discovered and used against it. They are not enemies of essential democracy, but of its illusions.

247. Propaganda working by the lie produces its own cure in a general education. At first it is answered by counter-propaganda, by counter-lies. But the people, in a conflict of lies, not only are found to doubt all propaganda, but to seek truth.

Propaganda itself, pretending to be truth, does not rely solely on the people's love of truth. It is more subtle. It is aimed partly at their love of wish-fulfilment—to make them feel safe, proud, and strong. But if it is known to be untrue, it fails of its chief effect in giving confidence or a sense of security. This failure is now common through Europe. Wherever there has been much propaganda, there is much disbelief.

Everyone knows how general is the mistrust, not only in Europe but throughout the world, of anything that seems like propaganda. Even bare news is doubted unless it can be checked.

248. A racial or nationalist faith while it triumphs is more exciting than drugs, but it has the same result. It produces a condition of nervous sensibility in which small affronts become unbearable and shock effects violent turns of feeling. The nationalist cannot bear to hear of a fault in his own people. He feels a bitter spite against any of them who fall below the ideal standard of his fancy. Should, then, the nation itself fail of his ideal or suffer some humiliation, he turns round and loathes it with that passionate hatred which is the obverse of passionate love. Everyone of us knows men who hate their native countries and abuse them with hysterical violence. These men, if they are sincere and whole men, all belong to one kind—those who as children have been taught lies about their country's glory. They were brought up on propaganda and now its wine has turned to vinegar.

249. This is true also in religion, and we have seen its effects in the last half-century. All the churches in the world have been attacked, and the bitterness of the attackers has astonished both men of free mind and priesthoods conscious of unselfish devotion to humanity. What difference, they ask, does it make to the virtue of Christ's spirit and example that scholars have thrown doubt upon the literal infallibility of the Bible ? We do not seek to teach man history

or facts about the Flood, but to give him the experience of God's grace—to make him know something much more important than historical fact, the joy of goodness, the transforming power of love. Why should men reject the fundamental truth of human sympathy because of a little primitive theology which they do not even understand ?

The answer is that men have always felt unreasonable hatred against those who even in innocence have betrayed their reason with lies or fears. It is true that millions avoid the churches out of laziness or indifference, but they do not hate them. You do not find church-burners and priest-haters in countries where the church is weak, but where it is strong. It is the devotees who burn and hate because they have been deceived.

Deception is a kind of oppression which, above all, is felt as a humiliation. A man would rather be known for a slave than a fool. Therefore deception of any kind, in education, in a state press, or a church creed, however dissembled in quibbling phrases, is probably the most dangerous trick of authority. If it is necessary for a dictator to deceive the people, so much the worse for him. What he has to hide is still working against him and his people are naked to surprise.

212

CHAPTER XIII

Education for Liberty, Specific

250. Education has been defined as controlled experience—instruction at home or in school, games, any reading chosen to give emotional or æsthetic experience, etc. Of this complete experience, teaching is usually considered separately, because it is factual and because the teacher is directly responsible for its effects.

251. A teacher does not draw out anything hidden in the child or remove restraint. He gives instruction which, with the rest of education, alters the child's ideas and therefore its character. He can do nothing without the child's co-operation * ; and he can do great harm by offering it experience or ideas which it cannot use or failing to give it those which it needs. But it will not form these ideas without him. It is by nature ready to accept almost anything that it is told, especially by a teacher it likes.

---

* The great value of W.E.A. classes is in this co-operation from willing learners. See *In Defence of Democracy*, Fulton and Morris, p. 178. Methuen, 1935.

If the ideas are false, incoherent, or unsuitable to its character, it will suffer, but it will not know the cause. For instance, at one time children used to be taught that for small crimes they would be sent to Hell and that a jealous God watched all their actions in order to catch them in a crime. Many could make no use of this instruction and did not attempt to do so. It only persuaded them that the world was a mysterious and irrational place beyond understanding. Others of unusual vitality—that is, of unusual power in all their instincts, unusual devotion, patience, and sincerity—entered strongly into the idea of Hell, of the jealous God, and the infallible Bible. Now, if devotion was their master instinct, they might become saints ; intolerant and oppressive, but in themselves good men. But if their instinct for truth had already by any accident fortified itself by the idea of truth, they were thrown into conflict. As their instincts and powers were strong, their conflict was violent and often produced religious melancholia or violent insanity.

But none of them blamed his teacher. They could not know what their lives might have been with a different imaginative scheme and different teaching.

A teacher, therefore, cannot escape responsibility for the results of his teaching. It is the necessary burden and glory of his creative art.

252. Education is founded on the belief that the child has power to learn, and that learning modifies its character and powers. Everyone, in fact, believes this. All teachers, all education, all people assume that children are free, that they have liberty in themselves— the power to know and to realize themselves.

253. Schemes to avoid the conflict of ideas by teaching all children the same things are based on a fallacy and produce evil or stagnation. For each child inherits different powers and acquires by a different total experience.* Among a hundred children given the same standard scheme, each will form a different personal idea. Countries with absolute education show precisely the same diversity of morals, manners, bitterness, spite, and moral degeneracy as democracies, as well as cynicism, hypocrisy, and despair peculiar to themselves. Even in politics and religion they cannot secure uniformity. This fact is obscured by the necessary hypocrisy of an absolute police state, but it is seen at once when the absolute authority breaks down.

Education, therefore, gains nothing by denying the fact of a child's unique quality. It must

* See "Heredity" : *Ency. Britt.*, Haldane.

treat each child as a free and distinct person, who cannot be deprived of his own private idea of the world. The child will form such an idea in any case, for it is a creative centre, and none or nothing can enter into his mind and create for it.

Methods of teaching, like those of Pestalozzi * and Montessori in modern times, based on this fact, have all had extraordinary success. Night classes, broadcast lectures, W.E.A. courses have the same reason for their good results, that those who use them do so only because they wish to learn.

This is not to exclude the duty of the state or the teacher. Education, no more than government, is *laisser-faire*. The experience which a Montessori school gives its children or a lecturer gives his class has to be devised for a purpose and paid for by society.

The final difference is not between men formed to a standard and those who have formed themselves, but between those who have formed different ideas, good or bad, false or true, from a total experience happening to them, of which the state and the school arrange what they can.

254. Men form ideas to realize their instincts. These are variously described or classified by different psychologists. Some, like

* Pestalozzi, 1746–1827.

Adler, make the creative instinct the master ; some, like Freud, the sexual ; some the tribal or co-operative ; some the pugnacious or competitive. Some perceive a separate æsthetic instinct in the love of colour, harmony, and pattern among children and certain animals. Some put it under other heads or derive it from tribal and sexual instincts. Freud believes that if the earliest ideas of a child, formed before it can speak, are in conflict, some may be suppressed out of conscious knowledge and produce neurosis. Some deny the unconscious memory of ideas. But all agree that instincts are realized in ideas and all under various names recognize in men impulses to seek knowledge, to act or create, and to love—which are realized in the countless forms of science, art, and religion, None of these is found in abstraction. The sciences use art and love in their ideas ; the arts use all the sciences ; religion uses science and all the arts as well as ideal devotion. The living person of a child or a man grasps them all into the general idea or ideas by which he directs his life, and by which he is directed.

255. A baby, for instance, finds itself part of a set of relations. It appears to itself the central focus of events like its mother, its meals, the sky, the grass, noises, and colours.

Some facts are in sight, some are only in

memory, but it puts them together to form its idea of a more complex set of relations. It knows that the back of its toy block, the nursery landing outside the door, nurse in the room beyond are there, and its mind grasps them into a single idea of the situation at the moment. Whether it takes the block, confident in its solid form, and throws it out of the window, confident that nurse will not see, depends upon this idea, which is a construction made up partly of seen facts, partly of unseen facts. It is not a real thing, but an idea of reality devised by the imagination.

But it does not throw the block to test the facts, but for pure enjoyment. To act, to use its power is a delight to it.

256. Children therefore want to know the truth, but only as a means to satisfy other instincts.* They take pleasure in learning facts, but not so much as in activity. Their whole life is activity, even when they sleep ; they want to be doing and all their deeds are grounded in imagination. The acts of a grown man, so far as they are willed and not purely instinctive, are intended to realize his ideas of honour, enjoyment, goodness, beauty, love, and even appetite.

257. Self-realization appears like a paradox.

---

* Unlucky little children are accused of lying when they are only making poetry of their experience.

How can anyone realize his own powers ? How can the self change itself ? But the fact is one of daily experience. Every man who says, "I will go into training for this race or game," or "I will learn the piano," changes the actual conformation of his body. He brings his muscles and nerves by a course of exercise to do things that they could not attempt before.

Without the liberty in the man, he could not realize himself. Just as Robinson Crusoe on his desert island possessed some liberty by right of birth, so every man possesses some power of self-realization in himself. Children marooned on a desert island would learn something : they would form a primitive language of grunts and gestures, and they would find out perhaps which plants were poisonous to them and how to make palæolithic weapons of rough stone. But seeing that mankind took many thousand years to discover the simplest crafts, they would not go far by their unaided powers.

Self-realization does not exclude the part of society in the man. A man, as realized person, owes almost all his integrated powers to society. But the essential power of integration and the personality itself are his own.

258. Ideas affect the body as well as the mind. A starving Mahometan could not eat pork, it would make him sick ; a navvy would

not be troubled with bird's-nest soup. As a musician or boxer in pursuit of his idea of excellence trains his muscle and changes the actual form of his body, so he also changes the powers of his mind. The boxer thinks more quickly ; the musician is able to grasp the idea of his music and to remember whole concertos.

259. An artist brought up to paint in a certain way and to think a certain kind of beauty the only true beauty cannot appreciate any other kind. If his style goes out of fashion, he does not say, "My idea of beauty is out of fashion," but "The world has gone mad and prefers ugliness to beauty." He can neither paint in the new style nor even understand it. Such artists, suddenly out of fashion, are often thrown into despair, so that they die broken-hearted. It seems to them not only that their lives have been wasted but that art itself has been destroyed. Their idea of beauty was part of them.

260. Men are not only formed by their imagination and limited by it in their scope of action, but they tend to love their own idea which they have made.

A religious man feels even more strongly than the artist a threat to his religion, in which he has created for himself so many noble and trans-porting images of goodness and beauty. A political man is enraged by the rebel who attacks that political scheme which represents for him not only security, peace of mind, the framework of his being, but the glory of his ideal country— the goodness and beauty of England, France, or Italy.

261. Men must have ideas to organize their lives ; but from the earliest childhood, long before they speak, they begin to be committed to them.

The ideas are often founded on lies or untruth. A child may begin with a conviction that all foreigners are wicked or that its own race is the greatest in the world. These are both ideas seized upon by the tribal instinct. An African farmer believes that human sacrifice is necessary for the fertility of his crops. Thus African farmers, some of the most good-natured people in the world, used to sacrifice slaves or war prisoners or their own children. A king of Spain expressed his pleasure in seeing heretics burnt. He was not a wicked man, but a dutiful one who had been taught young that God intended everlasting fire for all the unbaptized, and that to burn Jews alive was an act pleasing to God and his Jewish son.

Both these ideas are grounded in a belief now rejected. Human sacrifice does not improve crops and there is no evidence that Hell exists as a real place of fire. The idea of Hell cannot be disproved by facts ; it is not a lie. But it does not cohere with the general idea of the nature of reality founded on scientific discovery. We call it an untrue idea because if it were true then all science would be untrue. There are countless false ideas. The Hegelian theory of the state is one which has caused great misery in the world ; the anarchic theory is another, equally false and dangerous.

262. False ideas are especially dangerous to their holders, because they may lead them into conflict with facts. A man who believes that his nation is the greatest in the world may be confronted with facts, like defeat or a low standard of living. He has then the choice of inventing some fantasy to explain the facts away or despising facts altogether and committing himself to fantasy.

263. Children are often driven to fantasy by a conflict of ideas not only with facts but with each other. They have learnt incompatible ideas. A child who is told or who has overheard some trusted grown-up saying that everyone will be killed in the next war, that the war is inevitable, forms an idea which is incompatible with that of education. Why should he learn anything if he is going to be killed ? Why do his parents trouble about his education or his

manners ? His ideas fall into confusion and he either escapes into fantasy or gives up believing anything he hears. He becomes a neurotic or he joins the great number of those who have decided unconsciously that there is no truth anywhere in the world. He lives by his feelings, passes from one fantasy to another, and as a grown man swells the number of those who are prey to any spell-binder or nationalist quack.

264. Children, therefore, who begin with an innate love of facts and a desire for truth, come to believe lies and to act upon them. These false ideas produce conflict, persecution, civil wars.

But conflict also arises from ideas with an equal amount of truth or from ideas which do not need truth at all.

Scientists form different conceptions upon the same facts and quarrel about them. Artists realize in their works ideas which are concerned not with truth but with beauty. But quarrels about taste are unending, and a change of fashion in art causes loss and suffering.

The daily conflict throughout the world is a battle of ideas. Men seek power and fight for it, but they want the power to realize ideas. It is to maintain these ideas, to satisfy their love of them or to defend them, that civil and national wars are fought. A poor man does not

fight for bread or justice unless his mind has
formed the idea of poverty or injustice. Nations
do not fight for conquest or glory unless their
people or governments are moved by the
appropriate ideas. To change these ideas is
to change the policy of the nation. How far is
the conflict necessary and how far may teachers
seek to appease it ?

265. Conflict of ideas is of two kinds. It
arises from the idea itself or it does not. For
instance, the Japanese who believes that his
race is divinely appointed to rule the world must
fight all others with a similar nationalist idea.
He must seek to destroy them and their ideas.
But a scientist who believes that the search for
truth is the most important thing in the world
does not need to quarrel with another who differs
with him about the truth. One may think that
the world is made of little bits of matter ; the
other that it is a system of waves or vibrations.
Each has convincing proof. But both if they
are wise say, "Perhaps we are both wrong."

Conflict of scientific ideas does not arise from
the nature of science. It is implied by that
nature which is the search for facts, upon the
assumption that all the facts are not yet known.

266. In the same way, an artist who believes
that his own work is good and another's bad
does not need to hate or murder the other

224

artist. Art is purely ideal. It is not bound to any facts. Its variety and the conflict of tastes and fashions are therefore inevitable as long as artists are free to produce what they like.

Thus the conflict of scientists does not belong to the nature of science, which is the search for truth, and the quarrels of artists do not belong to that of art, which is their creative liberty acting in its proper function. Conflict and quarrels arise only when scientists regard their facts and ideas as final and when artists regard art as complete.

Toleration is essential to both because without toleration they contradict their own grounds of action, which are :

Science is not yet complete. Art can never be complete. } Thus all the ideal forms, so far as they are not false, have equal title to be respected.

That is to say, toleration belongs to the very idea of truth and the free mind seeking truth. Without toleration, the scientist will cut himself off from new facts and new ideas of truth.

267. Religion and politics, which use all the other ideas, are different in their realization. So far as they are not science and not art, and therefore not subject to the testing of facts or the comparison of artistic values, they are ideas about the ultimate reality.

225

Those ideas differ according to the temperament, education, and characters of persons. For example, millions of men believe that :

(1) God is a person who loves men and commands them to preach his message of love to the world, thus changing it from evil to good.

(2) God is an impersonal order caring nothing for men, who can only acquire happiness by retiring from the world, which is unchangeably evil.

(3) Universal war and competition are necessary functions of man, ordained by a higher power or process for his own pleasure or man's good.

(4) Peace and universal co-operation are necessary states of mankind, ordained by a higher power or natural order for man's happiness.

None of these ideas is grounded in facts demonstrably false. They arise from ideas which are either purely subjective and beyond test, or from scientific hypotheses based in some certain facts, like the evolutionary theory, the herd instinct ; and children take to them readily according to their natural powers and their experience. The first is, of course, more common in northern Europe, where the family experience is of parents with Christian ideas ; the second in the East. Children of a natural pugnacity or with a secret inferiority complex incline to the third. If it is presented to them they seize upon it as natural to their powers. Children of a naturally affectionate nature or those who suffer from the neuroses classified under the general heading of escape incline to the fourth.

268. So far as ideas are known to be false, no teacher should or can teach them. It is useless to say that a specific teacher may himself have false ideas and teach them, because it is obvious that he will do so. There are dogmatists also among the teachers, and there always will be. But in practice more truth is taught and less false ideas are taught now than twenty or perhaps even ten years ago.

The remedy for bad teaching where it exists is to improve the standards and pay of teachers.

The point here is not that false ideas may be taught, but that conflict may arise from ideas of equal truth ; or at least with equal rights to be considered true.

269. The conflict, as we saw, is in itself the means of progress not only of science but of politics and religion. All sects and parties are entitled to toleration. Therefore they are also entitled to education.

A teacher in combating a false idea does not merely deny it, but gives proof of its falsity.

To a child who has some false notion of race he points out that though there is a difference between races and though certain primitive tribes, now almost extinct, show inferiority, all the great branches of the human race now extant have equal excellence. It is in practice impossible to say which has given more or less to civilization.

270. To ideas not plainly false, however unpalatable or bizarre to his own feelings, he gives in the same way the fullest possible development. He gives to children power, so far as he can, to complete a coherent imagination of them and to see what they mean. For instance, he would encourage the non-resisting pacifist to recognize and face all the implications of his theory ; to understand the objections and meet them honestly ; and he would encourage the convinced militarist or believer in evolutionary competition to study its history and to realize its consequences.

271. In religion, if it were possible, a teacher of the child's own religion would give each child its truth without its falsehood. He must belong to that religion or he cannot give what is essential to it : the religious experience, the direct knowledge of God as known to that sect.

But if he belongs to the religion, so that he has

felt the revelation, he is very unlikely to distinguish between the different parts of its theology—those true to the religious insight and those false to fact. He is very unlikely to see that false facts which appear to him unimportant or which for himself he can explain away by some gloss are ruinous to the whole structure of faith.

272. The injury caused to a child's mind by confusion or reservation about the truth is incalculable, but in practice there is no direct cure for it. To abolish special religious teaching, if it were possible in a democracy, would do far more harm than good. The enemies of religion are more numerous and often more bigoted and dogmatic than its friends.

In practice, therefore, school-teachers can only do what they are doing : teach the love of goodness, sympathy, and honesty—which as a general idea answers a common instinct of all children—and with it the complementary ideas of toleration and truth.

273. The idea of toleration, which belongs to the nature of science and art and which is necessary to the existence and progress of all political and religious idea, arises from the nature of liberty. For if that power is real it produces new things, not only in art but science and religion. Therefore a man without toleration denies the liberty of man.

274. The idea of truth answers a common instinct of all children, and therefore it can be taught to all. But the instinct is not the idea, any more than the instinct to love is the idea of romantic devotion, loyalty, or self-sacrifice, which are built upon it. The child who wants to know does not perceive for himself any glory or virtue in seeking or maintaining truth. Still less can he understand that since truth is not complete, the idea of it must be grounded in toleration, that it must be expressed so : Truth is something that is valuable in itself ; it should be sought for its own sake. But it is not yet complete.

These general ideas of truth and toleration should govern all teaching. A teacher should say, "Here are the facts as I know them and the ideas based on them, but both may be wrong."

275. Experienced teachers say that no education is possible on this ground, that final truth is not known. They say that children must be given clear ideas and ask how clear ideas can be formed unless facts are given as true. They say also that children do not want to make up their own minds about facts and truth. They have neither time nor experience. They want something which feeds their imagination.

276. But the idea of toleration is itself a

true and clear idea which can be taught, and the idea of truth as the whole frame of things in their real being, meaning, purpose, and beauty is the most splendid that has ever seized upon the imagination of the greatest minds in the world. Those who have lived by that idea, from Socrates and Plato to Einstein and Whitehead, have not envied the Cæsars and Napoleons. They would not have changed the immense conquests and rich possessions of their ideas for those of any other. The imagination of Dante grasped a world in beauty, of Spinoza and Einstein a universe in one single coherent idea ; but Napoleon's idea was not even consistent with itself. His largest reach of fancy was to grasp Europe into an empire under his own dynasty. His ruling idea was glory and admiration, robes, crowns, medals—the triumph of a charade. He could realize his ideas only in complete independence of all other powers and at the same time in complete dependence upon the approbation of mobs. His purposes contradicted each other. He ended therefore in misery.

277. It is true that children like their ideas ready-made. They are in a hurry to use the ideas. If they are told that such and such a state is an enemy, they would rather hate that state and play at fighting it than stay to hear

some distinction between the state and its people. They will not puzzle out a doctrine of responsibility. Also they are quick to guess what a teacher or a parent himself is feeling and thinking, and they will take his ideas even when he tries to hide them. ·

It is true also that every man and teacher believes certain facts and certain ideas to be beyond doubt. He may say, for instance, "There are different opinions about the execution of Charles I," but he will declare with emphasis : "The revolution of 1688 was completely justified."

A teacher with no belief and no enthusiasm would be the worst teacher in the world. But let him believe in freedom and be enthusiastic for truth, and he will do no harm, for even if he teach some wrong facts or false ideas, he will also give the antidote.

For though children take their facts without examination and their ideas ready-made, if they are taught to respect facts and to love truth they have the power to correct themselves.

278. Children have all instincts in common. The difference of their characters is due to variety of temperament, of relative force in the instincts, of their inherited powers, and of those earliest ideas formed before their education begins.

But since all have common instincts, all can receive general ideas; not only the idea of truth, but of religion and of creative art. The general idea of religion is founded in the common instincts of love and compassion. The details of its expression and realization must and will follow the child's character, but as a general idea it can be given to all.

279. The idea of creation or construction is also a general idea answering a universal instinct. To teach children to love truth and goodness, to make things and enjoy making them, to know and enjoy all kinds of beauty, is no violence to inherited nature.

Some children seem indifferent to the arts. This is because they have already formed ideas inimical to the kind of art offered to them or because their taste is better than their teacher's. But all have æsthetic appreciation, because the act of imagination, by which the simplest forms are grasped in relation, is always accompanied by a feeling about the object. A child does not merely see the form and colour of a chair or try to grasp its solidity and use, he feels something about it—recognition, curiosity, like or dislike. It is probable that if he did not feel he would not be conscious of seeing it. The eye sees anything before it, but the brain only notices what it wants to notice. This feeling, when it is like or dislike of the object as an object, is æsthetic. It is beauty or ugliness. A child's favourite top or ball is beautiful to it except when it is using the thing as a weapon.

Those, therefore, who say "Ideas of truth and of goodness can be given to all children, but not ideas of beauty" are wrong. The æsthetic instinct is as primitive and universal as the other primary instincts.

280. But all these ideas must be given in their general form and grounded in the idea of the truth. For instance, to an art student a teacher would say, perhaps, "The truth is that all kinds of art have beauty and everything in the world can have beauty ; but that some concrete forms of art are richer in significance to some people. Paint and draw, therefore, what moves you personally, for only that can have beauty for you. If you are a trifling person, your art will be trifling. I can teach you technique and the means to realize your ideas in concrete form—drawing, painting, the use of mallet and chisel. I can show you all the concrete works of other artists, old and new, in order that you may see how they realized their ideas, and that you may perceive their ideas in their concrete richness. But I can't teach you a style or give you subjects."

In science, he says, "The truth is that all the

facts of this your subject are not known and no final truth is established. To go beyond the known facts is to stultify science. But if one of you prefers the quantum theory and another the wave theory, I have nothing to say. That is your own business, and you have liberty to form your own hypothetical ideas."

281. Simply because these ideas are general, they are often left unexpressed. Children are left to infer that truth is a value in itself, that duty and unselfishness are virtues, that beauty is made and found everywhere. But children do not infer things or easily form general ideas. Their minds are like sets of pigeon-holes, which may each contain a separate small idea totally unconnected with all the rest or with any general scheme. A child may know how the kittens were born, but know nothing of its own birth. It may think it right to be kind to so and so, but equally proper to hate somebody else. Thus notions of beauty commonly attach to single objects, so that each is a separate idea and there is no general principle at all. That is why grown men can totally fail even to see works of art as works of art, but are obliged to treat them as representatives of something else and to judge them on that ground.

Scientists who were not taught as children that the very idea of scientific truth is grounded in toleration carry their scientific conscience in one pocket and their dogmas in another.

General ideas, however obvious to a teacher, need statement to children in such form that they can be grasped.

282. But general ideas, even if expressed and grasped, do not avoid the conflict of opinion and tastes. Thus artists, though they know that everything can have beauty, still differ about the value of concrete works of art. The religious ideas of love, expressed in real life, produce violent difference of opinion, as when two parents for love of a child quarrel about its religious education. If they were indifferent or had no love, they would not quarrel. Unselfish duty is common to both sides in any civil war. The idea of the truth is the very ground of the battles of science.

To teach general ideas—of toleration, of truth, of love, beauty, and goodness—is not to escape the need of specific teaching in a chosen art, science, or religion, with the concrete details that differentiate it ; of a specific religious experience mediatized in a creed and acts of devotion. It cannot make all men agree. But that is to say, it cannot turn men into echoes or robots. It cannot remove from living reality the difference which is its actual life. It cannot destroy liberty, which is real creation.

Its function is to give liberty its full power.

Neither can it expect a solution of conflict even in the perfection of liberty. For the life of the world is real and the creative power of men is real. History is not an automatic progress hindered or helped by men. It is a true advance into novelty. Not merely the action of a great genius, but of every one of us, has effect upon the course of events. As we realize our ideas in concrete action, we make history.

Lessing called history the self-education of the world : that is, men learning from men and teaching men. It is certain that teachers, before all men, make history, because they create the creators.

283. Education gives liberty the full use of its reason, by which to realize its desires. Popular education results at first in nationalist egotism. But it brings its own cure, the only possible cure, by giving men power to understand that violence and intolerance are the chief enemies of their liberty.

CHAPTER XIV

Conclusion

284. This book was written in the spring of 1938. It is now November, and some people tell me that its arguments are wrong ; that democracy is already defeated. "It was an episode," they say ; "an accident of history between the collapse of the old patriarchal empires and the consolidation of the new, using scientific technique to produce and control slave states."

But history began in slave states, in brave new worlds, under tyrants and parties more absolute than any now seen. The juju priest, the god-king, the leopard society of Africa were once universal and their power was inconceivably great. They ruled by a terror which reached to the very souls of the people, and none dreamed of escape from it.

But the people broke off that rule. At first by imperceptible degrees, as a baby grows in knowledge and power unconsciously and blindly ; afterwards by sudden leaps of effort and discovery.

CONCLUSION

In the last century that irresistible growth of the peoples towards power terrified all the ruling parties and castes of the old world. They fought desperately against it. Metternich formed his Holy Alliance as an anti-democratic bloc which could call five million men into the field to crush revolution anywhere in Europe. It collapsed in the revolutions of 1848.

These revolutions marked the end of the old absolutism. They were followed by a new kind of device. The new Emperor Napoleon appealed to the people by plebiscite ; the English Government abolished the corn laws and extended the franchise ; the Tsar sought popularity by emancipating the serfs. Authority proposed to keep the people quiet by flattery and improved standards of life.

This method, followed in all countries, even more thoroughly in the old autocracies like Germany and Austria than in the democracies of the west, had great success in avoiding violence. But it did not check the growth of democracy. On the contrary, the people, given better wages, better education, pressed forward more rapidly. The revolution ceased to use violence, because it could go forward without it.

Thus the autocrats found themselves in a dilemma. Whether they opposed democracy by force or tried to kill it by kindness, the effect was the same.   Its power grew more formidable and their own weaker.

When they tried to divert it into imperialism, by throwing to the tribal passions of the monster the bouncing tub of glory, they had a world war.

285. But the war produced such a charge of liberty throughout the world as destroyed three empires and abolished a dozen monarchies. It quickened revolution in every country.

What we have seen in the last twenty years is the confusion produced by that sudden expansion of liberty, equivalent to the revolutions of a hundred years compressed into twenty. As in all sudden or violent revolution, it has been a time of extravagant hope and hysterical despair, wild projects, immense fertility of ideas good and bad, and groping, frightened governments ; while beneath this froth of noise and political nonsense the quiet millions, thinking, working, travelling, reading, formed their new ideas and realized some of them.

286. Meanwhile the old forces of reaction, justly terrified, have revived all the rallying cries of privilege, nationalism, racialism, imperialism, anti-semitism. The League has been broken and great democratic peoples have been brought under the absolute rule of police states.

But the check is superficial, because in spite

of it the organization of production, the spread of ideas, the improvement of transport, the devolution of real wealth go on everywhere—even in Spain during civil war and in Italy during foreign war. Real democracy, the power in the hands of the people, increases, and history shows that no autarch can finally ignore or divert that power. Even though he organize his state for production in order to strengthen his own position, he finds himself at last dependent on the will of producers.

Each check to democratic progress has been shorter than the last. It is not likely that this one can stand long against its immense weight. Jew-baiting is itself a symptom of that pressure in the autarchies. The Jews have always been the scapegoat of a secret police alarmed by revolutionary movement. But pogroms increase it by adding to it a moral sanction.

287. The common moral will of the world has great power, but the argument of this book is not that governments and peoples are morally bound to do certain things for the sake of liberty. It says, "Because liberty is a certain kind of free power in men, governments and peoples must do certain things or be broken."

288. Liberty, not by moral pressure alone, but by the total pressure of the free man,

inventive, persistent, adaptable, compels history to take this course :

Organization of peace and security within the state.

Organization of the state itself for the co-operative production and devolution of those powers of realization and enjoyment sought by men.

Organization of peace and security in the world.

Organization of world democracy for pro-duction and devolution to the national states of all their needs.

We see this process in mid-action. Even those who cannot see that it is the action of an implacable and invincible force, creative liberty itself, realize vaguely that there is some principle in history working against traditional power. They perceive that this force has lately taken new impetus throughout the world—in the remotest African villages, in Russia, India, China, among Japanese workers and Mongol herdsmen—and that every new invention of the free mind, aeroplanes, wireless, cheap pro-duction, cheap books, adds to it.

289. How long can any new alliance of frightened autarchies hold back the march of the peoples, gathering power from every check, recoiling upon their enemies with the enormous blind violence of war and revolution ?

CONCLUSION

Those who fight liberty set themselves against a power more subtle than thought ; as secret as will ; as persistent as nature, of which it is the life ; as all-pervading as life, of which it is spirit ; at a time when, throughout all countries of the world, it swells up towards the last phase of its revolutionary triumphs and the first of its world mastery.

CHAPTER XV

Summary of Chapters

Chapter I.

All men have power of voluntary action. This has produced mechanical and collective power, including that of states.

Man's power is not itself mechanical. It is creative and free. It is real liberty. Since liberty is real, democracy, which is power in many men, is also real. It is natural government. Anything which increases power in people increases real liberty and democracy. Education, industrial organization both increase democratic power. This power may not be at once effective in politics, but its pressure is always felt, even in an autarchy.

Chapter II.

Liberty is of the mind as well as the body. Moral freedom is not so important to the mind as freedom from prejudice. Children seek truth by nature. Man in this sense is born free. Since thoughts make acts, education is the key to liberty.

Mass education can succeed only among primitive or illiterate peoples. Even then it produces stagnation and injury to the state.

Chapter III.

Liberty has been defined as an absence of restraint. This definition is abstract and leads to confusion. Since liberty is real, it acts by itself, without regard to theory. In the nineteenth century while liberal theory conceived all government action as restraint, liberal governments pushed forward government action. They were increasing real liberty without perceiving it.

Power in men is of two kinds, unlimited and limited. Imagination and enjoyment are not necessarily limited, because they do not involve competition ; economic and political power have necessary limits. This fact has always led to conflict—man with man, and man with state.

Chapter IV.

Which is master, man or state ? Four types of answer have been given : (1) absolutist : the state shall be master—Plato, Hegel ; (2) anarchist : man is master—Proudhon, Tolstoy ; (3) both are masters—Rousseau ; (4) neither is master—Spencer and Marx.

245

Chapter V.

The question is insoluble in this form. It should be : By what standard can men and states be judged ? Such a standard or norm has been sought in law and the moral conscience. These are not true norms because not independent of opinion. True norms are measurements. The first, suggested by Bentham, was the greatest happiness of the greatest number. This failed because happiness could not be measured. The true norm must be a measure of liberty or power, the greatest liberty of the greatest number.

This standard is actually used in statistics of pay, leisure, education. These are all standards of liberty. They only need tabulation. But a norm cannot measure character. Its function is that of an average index, like those used by insurance brokers. It gives a standard of comparison. The basic figure in such a norm should be an index for political liberty.

Chapter VI.

Democracy arose from the primitive expansion of creative liberty producing conflict among the patriarchal families or tribes. The nearness of the masters compelled them to form national states and law. Cleisthenes and Solon invented the first democratic constitution and the vote.

SUMMARY OF CHAPTERS

Chapter VII.

Modern democratic organization is bureaucratic. This is inevitable. Yet bureaucracy is dangerous. The only effective check upon it is the group organization : into parties and into trade, professional, and play groups. The first make effective average opinion ; the second individual difference.

Chapter VIII.

Economic organization cannot be treated in abstraction. The unit is not the economic man, but the real man who uses his total power to modify economic conditions. Thus the structure of society, in spite of abstract economic or political ideas, is formed by human nature seeking realization : security, liberty, ownership.

Chapter IX.

Democracy is not a formula for security. It is something that exists and is growing in strength. It is stronger than autarchy, but it has dangers peculiar to it. These arise from the nature of liberty, in division of powers. Its chief weakness is in foreign policy. Its chief danger is therefore from outside, in war, which is due to international anarchy.

Chapter X.

The nearness of the patriarchs compelled them to agreement. The growing nearness of the sovereign states, due to improved transport, forced them to understanding and international agreement. Even before the war it produced the rudimentary organs of a world state. The war produced the League. It failed, but like Solon's first constitution it set before the world an idea to be realized of the democratic world state.

Chapter XI.

The chief enemy of world democracy is nationalism. It is natural to man and strengthened by prosperity. The problem is to decide the conflict between nationalist states. The people want peace. But peace cannot be secured without a supernational true law, sovereign over the world.

Chapter XII.

A child is formed by a total experience. This consists of environment and education. Environment is family, social, and national. Education is controlled experience, which includes teaching of facts. Total experience is therefore in three parts :

(1) Environment.
(2) Controlled experience, such as reading, games, plays, cinema, radio.
(3) Teaching.

Environment is partly real, partly spiritua.. The state is nowadays responsible for the chief part of it, housing, libraries, parks, etc. Also for the external spiritual atmosphere. This should be toleration. Toleration is not merely expedient, but the very ground of liberty, expressed so : "Because final truth is not known and never can be complete, all expressions of it have a right to be heard."

Truth is not stronger than lies, but more persistent. The only remedy in practice for lies and lying propaganda is toleration. All censorship is bad and dangerous in itself, especially in indirect forms like the English law of libel. Liberty of the press is essential not only to the people but the state, which can thus learn truth about opinion.

Chapter XIII.

Education is controlled experience at home and in school. Of this, teaching is a distinct part, because it is factual.

249

Schemes to avoid conflict of ideas by teaching children the same things are based on fallacy, and invariably fail. Education stands on the fact of a child's liberty, of a child's unique quality as a person.

Children seek facts, but only to realize their ideas. For this they need the full power of society. Yet the ideas are often in conflict. This conflict is inevitable. It is the result of creative liberty producing always a new situation, in art, science, religion, and politics. But conflict is the means of progress. All ideas are entitled to toleration. Toleration and truth are general ideas which can and must govern all education.

General ideas have to be stated. Children do not grasp them by nature. General religious ideas of charity, compassion, and love ; artistic ideas of beauty ; scientific ideas of the importance of truth, answer universal instincts. They can therefore form the basis of all education. Crude violence will disappear from the world not because conflict or variety of opinion and character come to an end, but because men in practice find disorder a check upon their liberty to create for themselves beauty and happiness. They forgo cheap and delusive triumph for the greater conquest of truth and honour.

Chapter XIV.

Attempted checks upon the advance of the democratic peoples have all failed. They produce only violence, war, or revolution. The last war caused an immense advance of liberty. To fight liberty is to oppose the power of nature itself.

CHAPTER XVI

Notes

290. Free will is a contradiction in terms, and that is why it cannot be proved. Will is purpose and purpose is not free. For instance, a man has a purpose to give sixpence to a beggar. Therefore his will, so far as it exists in an actual purpose, is committed to a certain action and it is not free. All actual purposes must appear as determined.

But free will is an abstraction. By freedom of the will people really mean the power in a man to do and think what he likes. Separate acts of will are the positive determinations of the man's liberty. He gives sixpence to the beggar because he wants to do so and has power to do so. The purpose is determined by him. It is not free, any more than a tool in his hand is free.

Have men liberty to form their own purposes and so to do what they like ? Can they create and invent, or are they automatic machines ? Did Dante, Shakespeare, Milton, Goethe originate anything, or were they barrel-organs ? If liberty is real in one man, it is real in all.

291. Everybody assumes liberty, but some

doubt the possibility of it. They do not see how it can exist in a world where everything is caused by something else. They say, "Everything that happens in the physical world is part of a chain of happenings and occurs according to fixed laws. How can man's action be an exception ?"

This objection to liberty is the strongest now existing, and it has actually caused many scientists, who use their own creative power every time they think or invent an hypothesis, to deny it and imagine themselves mere nerve centres.

It has caused some other scientists, revolting from this contradiction, to say that liberty, since it exists in men, must exist in atoms. They argue that the uniformity of nature is not real ; it is an average. The atoms of the two gases that form water need not really behave consistently, but when they are in a crowd they obey mob law.

292. This notion is rejected by such men as Einstein and Max Planck.* What is more, it is useless to solve the problem. For if crowds of atoms are determined, things made of those crowds are determined.

Neither would anyone, however devoted to liberty, thank you for a physical world of in-

* See Einstein's letter to Sir Herbert Samuel in *Philosophy and the Ordinary Man*, Appendix. Kegan Paul, 1932.

determinism. What would happen to liberty or the world itself if water chose to turn into fire or to run up-hill ; if a cricketer's bat turned into cotton-wool or an engineer's bridge into macaroni ? Life in such a world would be like playing croquet with flamingoes.

What we see in the real world is a continuous re-arrangement of material. The sculptor does not change the marble ; he carves it. The work of art is new, but the material is old. The inventor does not invent materials ; he puts them together in a new form. We don't say of a thing like stainless steel that so and so invented it. But we do say that so and so has invented a new machine.

293. The inventive mind continuously makes new things out of old materials. History, therefore, is like a tapestry made of coloured threads. Each thread is a continuous chain of determined events, of atomic movement. It is absolutely unbroken and eternal. It goes on for ever, in this world or another. But the creative mind weaves the threads into patterns which are always new and are never repeated. If the threads broke, the mind could not work ; but without the mind to weave the pattern, they would have no history.

294. This is an analogy. It explains only how creation can have liberty in determination

and how determination exists by creation. In fact, history is not pattern but the real life of creative being. The tapestry is both the artist and the work of art or, as we know it in ourselves, both the man and what he has made of himself.*

295. If a thing had no character, it would not exist. No one can even imagine a thing that is, but isn't anything. Neither can character have real existence without activity. It would be simply an idea, like a blue pig or a unicorn. A great philosopher has expressed this by saying, "It is not the case that there is an actual world which accidentally happens to exhibit an order of nature. There is an actual world because there is an order. If there were no order, there would be no world. Since there is a world, we know there is an order." †

296. Motion, time, life, mind, feeling, liberty, power are different names for the activity ; and the character is what we know as order, space, matter, body ; but the two cannot be separated in reality. Life doesn't exist without matter or mind without body. Liberty cannot exist without determinism or determinism without liberty.

297. When, therefore, we feel sure that we have real power to choose between different actions and to make new things, we are not

* See para. 257.
† A. N. Whitehead, Cambridge and Harvard. *Lowell Lectures*, 1926.

deceived. When a man says indignantly, "I know I have this power," he is quite right. He does know it, exactly as he knows when he has toothache.

No one can see a toothache, no one can even measure it. No one can see mind or life or the self or isolate them or put them into bottles. They cannot be isolated because they are abstract. It is not the mind that thinks or feels, but the man. It is not the body that disappears at death, but the spirit or character of the man. Thus we know that we have liberty exactly as we know that we are ourselves. A man who said "But I am not a self, I am nobody" may fairly be asked, "Who, then, is giving this opinion and what is it worth?"

Of one who denies liberty, we may ask, "If you have no power to judge anything, what is your judgment worth?"

298. Anarchists, autarchs, Marxians, Christians, Buddhists, and all scientists believe or assume that reality is a uniform single process.

Anarchists say, "There is a dialectic or process working through individual men to bring about a golden age of peace and co-operation."

Marxians believe in an economic process which will, unhindered, produce the good society.

For absolutists and Hegelians the process is spiritual or ideal.

Scientists see in nature a system uniform throughout. The elements in the stars are the same as those in the earth.

299. The universe is certainly a unity of some kind. It is either a fixed unity, in which all change is illusion, or a process. If it is a fixed, unchanging thing, then all our ideas are delusive. We do not really think or feel or act or live, for all these things take time. If we really live at all, we live in time ; in fact, as physicists say, we are made of space-time.

Reality is therefore a process in time. If we are real, we are part of a process ; we have a real past,* a real present, and we look forward to a real future, which is becoming real at every moment.

It is in fact quite impossible to suppose that we are not real, for if we suppose it, we must be real. Unreal beings can't think. Thought is the characteristic of a certain kind of organism.

300. But this process of history in which we live and of which we are part may carry us forward helplessly, like dead leaves in a stream. Many believe this to be so. They say, "There is creative power in the world process, but not in man."

There are two chief divisions in this faith : those who think the process blind and mechanical, a succession of events governed by some blind principle called evolution or causation ; and those who think that it is controlled by some transcendent god who says to man : "Don't think ; don't do anything by your own judgment. For I will guide your life."

In either case man's liberty is not real, and those who believe in process or guidance, though they are often political supporters of liberty, actually do great injury to democracy.

* A past, of course, which really only exists in the present as memory, education, heredity, etc., sustaining a character which does not pass but changes at varying rates and not continuously.

301. The first believe that the order of the process is impersonal ; the second that it is personal. Both include in their idea of order all experience—not only the scientist's experience of physical order, measured in quantities like centimetres, hours, degrees, foot-pounds, but qualities like appetite, instinct, colour, pleasure and pain, love and fear, goodness and beauty. The Christians say that brotherly love, which they find in nature, is good ; the Marxians say that friendly co-operation, which they find in nature, is good. They differ in other fundamental ideas, but they both find a quality in nature which they call good and which therefore implies a standard of good and evil.

Some believe that such a standard implies by itself a personal order. The others have two answers :

"Personality, whatever it is, arose from the inorganic and impersonal."

"If your God controls the world, why does he do it so badly ?"

302. Organism and mind were new things in history, but new things arise from the old. Professor Alexander explains how this might happen in his theory of emergence. He points out that the combination of elements may give a substance with entirely new and unexpected qualities. Water is made of gases, but it is not like gas.

So mind and personality could emerge from the inorganic.

303. It is true that organic life arises from inorganic elements. Certain elements are unstable and have what chemists call affinities for certain others. They join with those others if they can. Thus, under the right condition of temperature and light, the first organism emerges from the inorganic. It does so in the nature of things. There is no obvious reason why a scientist should not make life in a test-tube. It is only a more complicated task than causing water to arise from two gases. The water has entirely new and unexpected qualities of visibility, wetness ; organism has new and unexpected qualities of life, of renewing itself, of reproduction. Its kind of creation is different, at least in degree, from the blind or creative power of an element or a gas, which simply goes on creating itself by holding its electrons together in a certain order, and which grows only by addition. The organism grows by assimilation. Its self is not blind. Its feelings are different from those of elements. A piece of iron feels the influence of a magnet, but its reactions to the feeling are blind. The amœba reacts to feeling with purposive action—either to secure food or escape something unpleasant. The argument is that

a purposive self has come out of a blind order.

304. Those who believe in a personal order say what is undoubtedly true : "If purpose is anywhere in reality, it is part of natural order." What has happened when life and organism emerge from inorganic elements can only be explained by saying that there is a purpose in nature *which is always trying to emerge*. The affinity of certain elements is simply this effort seen from outside. Evolution is the history of this effort, and what Darwin calls the struggle for life is his description of it. Creatures want to live and to live more richly. The evolution of a man from the embryo might be called emergence. But no one thinks it a stroke of accident that a baby knows how to suck, that it grows teeth, begins to talk, to walk, to play, and ask questions. All that is called natural development and explained by heredity.

But the inorganic elements inherit. A gas is a perpetual inheritance of its own character. It inherits, too, the power and tendency to coalesce with certain others under certain conditions and to form compounds. So inorganic nature as a whole can be regarded simply as a stage of growth or development between two purposive beings : God and man. The stars are the seeds scattered, some on stony ground and some on the fertile. The lucky ones grow, but not by luck. They fulfil and realize their being.

305. The objection that the world, as we know it, does not look like a self-conscious being is anthropomorphic. No one supposes that an eternal God existing in all space-time for ever is like a man. A microbe in the human body might say, "I see millions of cells in every stage of life, some living, some prosperous, some dying or dead ; and much rubbish, organic and inorganic, lying about everywhere, very much in the way. The living cells are certainly highly purposive and busy creatures. I scarcely know what they'll be at next ; but they're always busy and pushing, arranging and re-arranging the rubbish, marrying and giving in marriage, reproducing themselves, eating, organizing. Many of them prove wasters, get into trouble, make a mess of things, and die young. I never saw such a turmoil. But all this talk about a superior being who includes them or who acts or feels through them is utter nonsense. Where and what is he ? Who ever saw him ? There is not the slightest evidence or need for his existence. He could not even communicate with these cells in the blood-stream, my good friends whose patronage supports my humble needs. They are divided by huge spaces

through which I stroll when I choose. He is not, I presume, on the telephone. The notion of a man is pure mythology and superstition."

The argument from appearance is not any better than the argument from experience. It is perhaps not so strong.

306. What is called the problem of evil is a more important objection. Evil and frustration are daily experience. If God made the world, why did he make evil ?

The usual answer is that God wishes men to be good and that they can't be good unless they have the power to be evil.

This fails to convince anyone not anxious to be convinced, because it still makes God responsible for evil.* He allows it for a good end, perhaps ; but would we admire a nurse who took away the nursery fire-guard to please herself with the idea of the children's prudence in not being burnt alive ?

It would be easier to believe what we see every day, that God's will is limited by obstacles which arise naturally, that evil exists because creative liberty is real, and because God really exists. Real existence in space-time involves limitation. That is, God could not abolish the evil that men do without abolishing man's

---

* Moralists and theologians therefore use it at their peril

liberty ; but that is to abolish his own creative power. If liberty, the power of the cells, is necessary to the existence of man, the liberty of all nature is necessary to the real existence of God.

God in that case would not be responsible for the evil of the real world.* He would struggle with it as a man struggles to realize his own good will against limitations which are in his own real being. That struggle would then be the proof of God's real existence.

307. Thus those who believe in the personal God and those who believe in impersonal process can each be right, and the argument between theists and atheists is not really one between those who believe in liberty and those who don't. Both sides can equally deny liberty according to their conception of the actual working of God or process in the world.

308. The theory of automatic progress is the foundation of much political theory. *Laisser-faire* arose from it. It was strengthened by the proof of evolution and talk about the laws of nature.

These laws are imagined as governing man and things from outside. They suggest the

* Omnipotence in theology means "power to do all that is possible," not "power to do everything."

idea of men and things as dependent on some outside rule, which as process commands their fate, or as God guides them.

But nature has no laws. There are no policemen in space directing the traffic of the stars. No rule compels a seed to grow. Seeds grow because of something inside them which looks for and finds something outside them which they can use. Elements behave in a certain manner because it is their way. If it was different, they would be different. Physical nature is the character of life, the way it behaves. It is highly complex, but its character is uniform. It does not need laws to make it behave like itself, even if anyone could be imagined outside reality giving laws to real being.

There is no law of evolution. It resembles a growth or development. This growth culminated, after much groping, in man's reason.

Reason enabled man to survive because it gave him control of his environment.

309. The difference between a creature with instinct and man with reason is that the former is limited to a tribal or collective action. Its liberty is only to repeat. It cannot vary its conduct, and therefore its hereditary tribal skill in doing exactly right in fixed conditions is bound up with its failure to adapt itself to a change of conditions. The skill and the failure

are two limits or characteristics of the same thing : instinctive action.

310. Man with reason is born ignorant. He is therefore adaptable to circumstances. He learns the world anew, and if it is a changed world, he has a changed knowledge and can change his action. But since he is born ignorant, he can learn wrongly ; and since by reason he can study a situation and do right in it, he can also do wrong.

311. For man, therefore, progress depends on the use of his reason. He realizes for himself his instinctive desires, what we call his nature, by the use of independent judgment. That is his means and his only means of self-development.

Whether the reason is God's seeking to realize his love, wisdom, and delight in concrete existence or whether it is the product of blind luck, it must have liberty or it cannot do its work. It has evolved creative liberty only for the purpose of independence and adaptability.

312. This, then, is the vital distinction. All sects and political parties believe in a unity which is realized in the process of history. But some say the process is automatic and does not need the use of human judgment ; others say : "The process is achieved by the use of reason and judgment, and therefore it is not automatic."

313. But the first contradict themselves. For they deny reason with reason. To look for guidance in anything but reason, to trust some innate blind principle or automatic process is for an atheist to deny the only means of progress and for the theist to abandon God himself in his own essential action.

Index

269

INDEX

INDEX

271

INDEX

INDEX

INDEX

DATE DUE

AP 12 77			
GAYLORD			PRINTED IN U.S.A.